NEW Cornerstone

WORKBOOK

3

T0344124

New Cornerstone 3
Workbook

Pearson, 221 River Street, Hoboken, NJ 07030
Cover Credit: Alphaspirit/123RF

Printed in the United States of America

ISBN-13: 978-0-13-523463-1
ISBN-10: 0-13-523463-8
27 2022

www.english.com/cornerstone

Contents

Unit 1

Unit 2

Unit 3

Contents

Name _____   Date _____

Key Words

Use with Student Edition pages 8–9.

street
flower
luck
letter
greet

A. **Find the Key Word from the box that completes each sentence. Write the word.**

1. With a little _____,
I will win the race!

2. Let's pick a _____ from
the garden.

3. Haley enjoys writing a _____ to her
grandmother.

4. There are many cars driving on the _____.

5. It is polite to _____ someone when they
come to your house.

B. **Unscramble the letters to form a Key Word.**

6. e t l r t e _____

7. k u l c _____

8. t t r e e s _____

9. w o r f e l _____

10. t e g e r _____

3

Academic Words

Use with Student Edition page 10.

A. Read each clue. Find the Academic Word in the row of letters. Then circle the word.

1. buy   k m z p u r c h a s e g n w

2. single piece or thing   d b c o n s i t e m a p l y r

B. Write the Academic Word that *best* completes each sentence.

3. I will _____ new shoes.

4. Each _____ in the store was on sale.

5. Mom will _____ food at the store.

6. This t-shirt is my favorite _____ of clothing.

C. Answer the questions.

7. Name something you would like to **purchase**.

_____

8. What is your favorite **item** of clothing?

_____

Copyright © 2019 Pearson Education, Inc.

Home-School Connection   Take a walk in your neighborhood with a family member. Talk about what you see. Use the academic words.

Name _____ Date _____

Phonics: Short Vowels

Use with Student Edition page 11.

> A word may have a short vowel when it has a consonant-vowel-consonant pattern.
>
> c a t
C V C

A. **Fill in the blank with a vowel to make a CVC word. Some examples have more than one choice.**

1. v _____ n

4. h _____ t

2. b _____ d

5. c _____ t

3. l _____ p

6. b _____ s

B. **Circle the CVC words with a short vowel.**

7. I can run all the way home.

8. We can have fun at the park.

9. Please let me stay up late.

10. The baby can sit up.

Home-School Connection List two more CVC words with each vowel.
Read your words to a family member.

Comprehension: *Lin's Shopping Day*

Use with Student Edition pages 12–15.

Answer the questions about the reading.

Recall

1. Where do Lin and her dad stop first?

   _____

2. What type of cabbage makes Mom happy?

   _____

3. What does the mail carrier drop?

   _____

Comprehend

4. Why does Lin pinch her nose?

   _____

   _____

   _____

Analyze

5. Why does Lin buy her mom bok choy?

   _____

   _____

   _____

Name _____ Date _____

Reader's Companion

Use with Student Edition pages 12–15.

Lin's Shopping Day

Lin jumps from the bus onto the street.

With so many people, she must move her feet.
Dad quickly takes hold of Lin's little hand.
The first stop on their list is a smelly fish stand.

Lin takes a sniff and pinches her nose.
She can see lobsters if she stands on her toes.
Next on their list is a store that sells flowers.
Lin tells Dad she could smell them for hours.

Use What You Know

List three people you know in your neighborhood.

1. _____

2. _____

3. _____

Reading Strategy

Tell one thing you know about Lin. Underline the clue that shows this.

Genre

Many poems have words that rhyme, like *street* and *feet*. Circle two other pairs of words that rhyme.

Use the Strategy

Do you think Lin likes living in her city? Explain why or why not.

_____

_____

_____

Retell It!

Retell this passage as if you are Lin. Tell a friend what you did.

_____

_____

_____

_____

Reader's Response

Pretend you are in Lin's city. What would you like to do?

_____

_____

_____

Home-School Connection Retell the passage to a family member.

Name _____   Date _____

Learning Strategies: Understand Character
Use with Student Edition pages 16–17.

Read the passage. Look for clues that tell you about the character. Answer the questions.

Joy's Job

Joy has a job. She takes her neighbor's dog for a walk. She walks the dog each afternoon when she comes home from school. She takes the dog to the park. Then she brings the dog home. She gives it food and water.

1. List three things that Joy does on her job.

_____

_____

_____

2. Which sentence *best* describes what Joy is like? Circle the letter of the correct answer.

A Joy is a good student.

B Joy is good at her job.

C Joy is a friendly person.

D Joy likes to go to the park.

Home-School Connection

Pick a character in a book or TV show. Tell a family member what the character is like.

Grammar Simple Present: *Be* Verbs

Use with Student Edition pages 18–19.

These are the different forms of *be*.

am	are	is

A. Write the correct form of the *be* verb to complete each sentence.

1. Joe and Juan _____ at school.

2. Maria _____ on the swim team.

3. I _____ nine years old.

4. We _____ on the bus.

5. He _____ at school.

B. Write the contraction to complete each sentence.

1. (He is) _____ in third grade.

2. (I am) _____ very tall.

3. (We are) _____ in the city.

4. (You are) _____ in the class.

5. (They are) _____ at the movies.

6. (She is) _____ riding her bike.

7. (It is) _____ time to eat.

8. (We are) _____ reading a book.

Home-School Connection Write two sentences. Use *is* and *are*. Read the sentences to a family member.

Name _____ Date _____

Spelling: CVC Words

Use with Student Edition pages 20–21.

A. Fill in the blank with *a, e, i, o,* or *u*.

1. m _____ n   m _____ n

2. c _____ p   c _____ p   c _____ p

3. d _____ g   d _____ g   d _____ g

B. Fill in the blank with a consonant. The examples have many choices.

4. _____ o g   _____ o g

5. r u _____   r u _____

 Write three sentences using CVC words.

_____

_____

_____

Home-School Connection   Write one CVC word with each vowel. Read your words to a family member.

Writing: Describe a Person

Read the paragraph. Then read each question. Circle the letter of the correct answer.

(1) My mother is friendly. (2) She says hi to peple and smiles at them. (3) Our neighbor, Mrs. King, lives alone. (4) My mother visits her every afternoon. (5) Mrs. King says my mother are the kindest woman she knows. (6) My mother spends a lot of time with me. (7) She and I talk a lot. (8) She is very patient and loving. (9) She is a great mom!

1. What change, if any, should be made to sentence 2?
   A Change *smiles* to *smile*
   B Change *peple* to *people*
   C Change *She* to *she*
   D Make no change

2. What change, if any, should be made to sentence 5?
   A Change *Mrs.* to *Mrs*
   B Change *says* to *say*
   C Change *are* to *is*
   D Make no change

3. What change, if any, should be made to sentence 6?
   A Change *spends* to *spend*
   B Change *me* to *I*
   C Change *time* to *tiem*
   D Make no change

Name _____ Date _____

Key Words

Use with Student Edition pages 22–23.

A. Find the Key Word from the box that completes each sentence. Write the word.

1. I like to eat cake

   for _____.

2. I will _____ milk and eggs in a bowl.

3. My best _____ Rosa will be at my party.

4. I can _____ my clothes and put them away.

B. Circle the Key Words in the Word Search.

F	R	I	E	N	D	T
X	K	O	I	N	E	D
C	Q	A	W	X	S	M
R	F	N	I	A	S	E
W	O	M	T	K	E	U
C	L	E	L	Z	R	R
D	D	Y	Z	E	T	F

Academic Words

Use with Student Edition page 24.

A. Read each clue. Find the Academic Word in the row of letters. Then circle the word.

1. make something   k m z p u r c r e a t e k l p t

2. job that must be done   d b c o n s i t a s k a p l y r

B. Write the Academic Word that *best* completes each sentence.

3. We _____ art in art class.

4. I can _____ a paper airplane.

5. My _____ is feeding the dog.

6. The teacher gave us each a _____ .

C. Answer the questions.

7. Name a **task** you have at home.

_____

8. What is your favorite thing to **create**?

_____

Home-School Connection   Use each Academic Word in a sentence. Read your sentences to a family member.

Name _____ Date _____

Phonics: Long Vowels with Silent e
Use with Student Edition page 25.

Choose the word from the box that *best* completes each sentence. Write the word.

bake	close	five	hope	like
mice	ride	same	slide	snake

1. Sam and I have the _____ book.

2. Cats eat _____ .

3. I like to go down the _____ .

4. We _____ our team will win.

5. Can we _____ cookies for my birthday?

6. Mari and Rose want to _____ a horse.

7. Jake saw a _____ in the grass.

8. There are _____ children at our table.

9. Please _____ the door.

Home-School Connection Find three more words in a book with a long vowel and silent *e*. Read your words to a family member.

Comprehension: *Making Friends*

Use with Student Edition pages 26–31.

Answer the questions about the reading.

Recall

1. Where is Hana from?

_____

2. What is a crane?

_____

3. What did Carlos make?

_____

Comprehend

4. How did his mother help him?

_____

_____

_____

Analyze

5. How did Hana and Carlos help each other?

_____

_____

_____

Name _____ Date _____

Reader's Companion

Use with Student Edition pages 26–31.

Making Friends

Hana just came to this school. She is from Japan. Hana does not have a friend yet.

Carlos just came here. He is from Mexico. Carlos does not have a friend yet.

Miss Jones tells Carlos to sit by Hana. She asks Hana to teach a fun thing to Carlos. Hana says she can make paper animals. Her mother showed her how. Carlos thinks that is a fun thing to do.

Use What You Know

List the names of three of your friends.

1. _____

2. _____

3. _____

Reading Strategy

What do you think Hana will teach to Carlos? Underline the clue that tells this.

Comprehension Check

Why don't Hana and Carlos have friends? Circle the sentences that tell why.

Use the Strategy

List two events that happen in the passage. Put them in the right order.

_____

_____

_____

Retell It!

Retell this passage. Pretend you are Hana. Tell a parent about what happened at school.

_____

_____

_____

_____

_____

Reader's Response

What fun thing can you do? What can you teach to a friend?

_____

_____

_____

Home-School Connection   Retell the passage to a family member.

Name _____ Date _____

Learning Strategies: Sequence of Events

Use with Student Edition pages 32–33.

**Read the passage. Then read the list of events. Write *1, 2, 3, 4,*
and *5* to show the sequence.**

Play Ball!

Leon and Gina play with a ball in the park. Leon throws the
ball to Gina. Gina throws the ball to Leon.

Leon tries to catch the ball. He misses it. A dog runs and picks
up the ball. Gina and Leon chase the dog. But the dog runs away
with the ball!

_____ Gina and Leon chase the dog.

_____ Leon misses the ball.

_____ Gina throws the ball.

_____ Leon throws the ball.

_____ The dog picks up the ball.

🏠 **Home-School Connection** | **Read the events in the right order. Make up what happens next.
Share your idea with a family member.**

Grammar: Simple Present

Use with Student Edition pages 34–35.

Verbs in the simple present tell what usually happens. They change form to agree with the subject.

I see the bird.	Hana sees the bird.	Hana and Carlos see the bird.

A. Circle the verb.

1. Hana goes to school.

2. Carlos sits with Hana.

3. The children play outside.

4. Miss Jones reads a story.

5. Maria and Kate eat lunch.

B. Choose the correct verb. Write it on the line.

6. Mom _____ dinner. (cook, cooks)

7. Jason and Dad _____ dessert. (make, makes)

8. The dog _____ the ball. (get, gets)

9. Mayda and I _____ to the store. (walk, walks)

Home-School Connection

Make a list of five verbs. Act them out for your family. See if your family members can guess the verb.

Name _____   Date _____

Spelling: Proper Nouns
Use with Student Edition pages 36–37.

A. Fill in the blank with a proper noun.

1. My best friend is _____ .

2. My teacher's name is _____ .

3. The name of my school is _____ .

4. This month is _____ .

5. My favorite holiday is _____ .

6. The town we live in is _____ .

7. The country we live in is _____ .

8. My favorite day of the week is _____ .

 Write three sentences. Use a proper noun in each sentence.

_____

_____

_____

Home-School Connection   List three proper nouns. Share your list with a family member.

21

Writing: Describe a Sunny Day

Read the paragraph. Then read each question. Circle the letter of the correct answer.

(1) On a sunny day, I go to the park near my apartment. (2) My sister, Liliana, and I plays. (3) Our grandmother, Abuela, sits on a bench and watches us. (4) Later, the ice cream truck arrives. (5) Liliana and me race to be first. (6) I ask for chocolate. (7) Liliana's favorite is strawberry. (8) As we walk home, I smell flowers and grass. (9) I love these sunny days.

1. What change, if any, should be made to sentence 2?
   A Change *plays* to *play*
   B Change *sister* to *Sister*
   C Change *I* to *me*
   D Make no change

2. What change, if any, should be made to sentence 4?
   A Change *ice cream* to *ice creem*
   B Change *arrives* to *arrive*
   C Change *Later* to *later*
   D Make no change

3. What change, if any, should be made to sentence 5?
   A Change *me* to *I*
   B Change *race* to *races*
   C Change *first* to *ferst*
   D Make no change

Name _____ Date _____

Key Words

Use with Student Edition pages 38–39.

celebrate

crowd

company

weekend

gathers

A. Find the Key Word in the box that completes each sentence. Write the word.

1. Do you like it when _____ comes to your house?

2. The family _____ together to eat dinner.

3. Anna and Luis _____ when they make good grades.

4. There was a big _____ at the game.

5. Rosa plays with her friends on the _____.

B. Write the Key Word from the box that *best* matches the clue.

6. Saturday and Sunday _____

7. big group of people _____

8. comes together _____

9. do something special _____

10. friends that come over _____

Academic Words

Use with Student Edition page 40.

A. Read each clue. Find the Academic Word in the row of letters. Then circle the word.

1. give something   c o n t r i b u t e a t e k l p t

2. almost the same   d b c o n s i m i l a r l n g l t

B. Write the Academic Word that *best* completes each sentence.

3. Maria and Josie's shirts were _____.

4. We will _____ to the animal shelter.

5. Mom will _____ time in the library.

6. The dogs looked _____.

C. Answer the questions.

7. Name two things that are **similar**.

_____

8. How can you **contribute** to classroom clean-up time?

_____

Home-School Connection   Use the Academic Words to a write a story about a special day. Read your story to a family member.

Name _____ Date _____

Word Study: Use a Dictionary
Use with Student Edition page 41.

You can look up words in a dictionary to find out what they mean. Some words have more than one meaning.

Read each sentence. Look at the underlined word. Then circle the letter of the *best* meaning for the underlined word.

1. Children like to <u>play</u> with toys.

    A performance on a stage

    B have fun with

2. The rocket zoomed up into <u>space</u>.

    A area past Earth

    B place where you can put something

3. I read <u>a lot</u> of books last summer.

    A area of land

    B large number

4. A whale has a very big <u>mouth</u>.

    A place where a river enters the ocean

    B body part used for speaking and eating

Home-School Connection

Look up the word *right* in a dictionary. Write two sentences using two different meanings of the word. Share your sentences with a family member.

Comprehension: *My Family*

Use with Student Edition pages 42–47.

Answer the questions about the reading.

Recall

1. What does the family do on the weekend?

_____

2. What do they celebrate?

_____

3. What is on top of the cake?

_____

Comprehend

4. How does the family plan the party?

_____

_____

_____

Analyze

5. Why are family celebrations fun?

_____

_____

_____

Name _____ Date _____

Reader's Companion

Use with Student Edition pages 42–47.

My Family

Sometimes, friends join our family celebrations. Company gathers in our yard. Neighbors, friends, and family come over. There is a big crowd.

Everyone brings something to the party. There is plenty of food. Dad cooks. Mom makes salad. We drink lemonade. We eat dessert.

We laugh and talk. We play games and have fun. You can tell that we are having a good time. I like to see everyone together.

Use What You Know

List three people in your family.

1. _____

2. _____

3. _____

Reading Strategy

List three foods your family eats on special days.

1. _____

2. _____

3. _____

Comprehension Check

Circle two things the family in the passage eats.

MARK THE TEXT

Use the Strategy

Describe a game you play with members of your family.

_____

_____

_____

Retell It!

Pretend you were at the celebration described in the passage.
Tell what happened.

_____

_____

_____

_____

Reader's Response

When do you think this celebration took place? Why do you
think that?

_____

_____

_____

Home-School Connection Retell the passage to a family member.

Name _____ Date _____

Learning Strategies: Make Connections

Use with Student Edition pages 50–51.

Read the passage. Then answer the questions.

Weekends at My House

Each weekend is the same. My brother and I want to sleep late. But Dad wakes us up early. He has plans. "I know you guys want to help out!" he says.

Last weekend, my brother and I helped Dad paint. Two weekends ago, we worked in the garden. What will we do this weekend? Dad says the garage looks messy. I know what we will do this weekend!

1. What do you do on the weekends?

_____

_____

2. How do you help out at home?

_____

_____

Home-School Connection   **Read your answers to a family member.**

Grammar Nouns: Singular and Plural

Use with Student Edition pages 52–53.

most nouns, add **-s**	candle ⟶ candles
nouns ending in: *-s, -ss, -ch, -sh,* or *-x*, add **-es**	wish ⟶ wishes
nouns ending in vowel + consonant + *-y*, change the **-y** to *-i* and add **-es**	family ⟶ families
Irregular nouns, **look them up in a dictionary**	child ⟶ children

Complete each sentence. Use the plural form of the noun. Write it on the line.

1. candle   I put eight _____ on the cake.

2. dish   Mother washed _____ in the sink.

3. flower   Lupe put _____ in a vase.

4. dress   Angie packed two _____ for her trip.

5. bus   Dad takes two _____ to work.

6. baby   We heard _____ laughing.

7. leg   A dog has four _____.

8. child   There are six _____ in my group.

9. box   She needs six _____ for her toys.

10. inch   I am four feet and six _____ tall.

Home-School Connection

Make a list of five nouns. Write the plurals. Read them to your family.

Name _____ Date _____

Spelling: Plural Nouns

Use with Student Edition pages 54–55.

Write the plural form of each word.

1. city   _____

2. bus   _____

3. kiss   _____

4. fox   _____

5. lady   _____

6. fish   _____

7. lunch   _____

Write a story about your family. Use three plural nouns.

_____

_____

_____

_____

Home-School Connection   **Read your story to a family member.**

Writing: Describe a Family Celebration

Read the paragraph. Then read each question. Circle the letter of the correct answer.

   (1) Every year, we have a birthday party for my grandfather. (2) The hole family works together. (3) My cousins put flower around the house. (4) My aunts make a beautiful cake. (5) My sisters put candles on the cake. (6) My brothers put up balloons in the living room. (7) Then we hide. (8) We hear my grandfather's feet on the front porch. (9) When he opens the door, we yell, "Surprise!"

1. What change, if any, should be made to sentence 2?
   A Change *hole* to *whole*
   B Change *works* to *work*
   C Change *family* to *families*
   D Make no change

2. What change, if any, should be made to sentence 3?
   A Change *cousins* to *cusins*
   B Change *put* to *puts*
   C Change *flower* to *flowers*
   D Make no change

3. What change, if any, should be made to sentence 5?
   A Change *put* to *puts*
   B Change *My* to *my*
   C Change . to ?
   D Make no change

Name _____ Date _____

Review

Use with Student Edition pages 2–55.

Answer the questions after reading Unit 1. You can go back and reread to help find the answers.

1. In *Lin's Shopping Day*, how do you know that Lin is friendly?

_____

_____

2. What do you learn about Lin from these sentences? Circle the letter of the correct answer.

> Lin says she's sorry, and helps him repack,
> then Dad says it's time to go buy a snack.

A Lin is helpful.
B Lin works for the post office.
C Lin only buys snacks with Dad.
D Lin wants to mail a letter.

3. In *Making Friends*, which event happens first? Circle the letter of the correct answer.

A Hana teaches Carlos how to make a paper crane.
B Miss Jones tells Carlos to sit by Hana.
C Carlos and Hana help make a dessert.
D The other girls and boys taste the dessert.

4. How do Hana and Carlos change during the story? Circle the letter of the correct answer.

   A At first they are happy. At the end they are sad.
   B At first they are sad. At the end they are happy.
   C Hana learns how to make a paper crane.
   D Carlos learns how to make a dessert.

5. In *My Family*, how does the family celebrate the grandmother's birthday?

_____

_____

6. Read these sentences from *My Family*.

> Neighbors, friends, and family come over. There is a big crowd.

What does **crowd** mean? Circle the letter of the correct answer.

   A one person
   B family
   C a lot of people
   D children

7. Describe one thing your family does that is similar to the family in the selection.

_____

_____

Home-School Connection | Tell a family member something new you learned in this unit.

Name _____ Date _____

Writing Workshop: Describe an Event

Read the passage. Then read each question. Circle the letter of the correct answer.

The Class Picnic

(1) Our teacher, Miss Jones, has a big surprise. (2) "Tell us!" we shout. (3) She says, "We will go on a picnic."

(4) We bring our lunches. (5) Miss Jones brings cookies and lemonade.

(6) At noon we walk to the park. (7) Miss Jones spreds out a cloth. (8) We sit down. (9) We eat our lunchs.

(10) After lunch we go to the playground. (11) Some children like the swings. (12) Other children like to climb the ropes.

(13) When Miss Jones has another idea. (14) We get into teams. (15) We play *Hide and Seek*. (16) We have fun on our picnic.

1. What change, if any, should be made to sentence 1?

   A Change *surprise* to *surprises*

   B Change *teacher* to *Teacher*

   C Change *teacher,* to *teacher*

   D Make no change

Circle the correct answer.

2. What change, if any, should be made to sentence 7?

    A Change *spreds* to *spreads*

    B Change *Miss Jones* to *miss Jones*

    C Change . to ?

    D Make no change

3. What change, if any, should be made to sentence 9?

    A Change *eat* to *ate*

    B Change *lunchs* to *lunches*

    C Change *our* to *Our*

    D Make no change

4. What is the **best** way to combine sentences 8 and 9?

    A We sit down but we eat our lunches.

    B We sit and eat our lunches down.

    C We sit down, and we eat our lunches.

    D We eat our lunches and we sit down.

5. What change, if any, should be made to sentence 13?

    A Change *When* to *Then*

    B Change *has* to *have*

    C Change *idea* to *ideas*

    D Make no change

Name _____ Date _____

Fluency

Use with Student Edition page 63.

How fast do you read? Use a clock. Read the text about *My Family*. How long did it take you? Write your time in the chart. Read three times.

I like it when my family gets together on weekends	10
We talk, laugh, and play games. There is plenty of	20
food to eat. There is plenty of noise! You can tell that	32
everyone is happy to be together.	38
Sometimes, we celebrate a special day. For my	46
grandmother's birthday, we all work together to plan	54
her party. We put up streamers, make a cake, and get	65
a gift. We all sing the birthday song, too. Our family	76
celebrations are so special!	80

My Times

Learning Checklist

Check off what you have learned well. Review if needed.

Word Study and Phonics

☐ Short Vowels

☐ Long Vowels with Silent *e*

☐ Use a Dictionary

Strategies

☐ Understand Character

☐ Preview

☐ Sequence of Events

☐ Make Connections

Grammar

☐ Simple Present: *be* Verbs

☐ Simple Present

☐ Nouns: Singular and Plural

Writing

☐ Describe a Person

☐ Describe a Sunny Day

☐ Describe a Family Celebration

☐ Writing Workshop: Describe an Event

Listening and Speaking

☐ Play a Description Guessing Game

Name _____ Date _____

Test Preparation

Use with Student Edition pages 64–65.

Read and answer the question below. Mark the space for the answer you have chosen.

1. This is a _____.
   ○ turtle
   ○ clock
   ○ flower
   ○ baseball

Read this selection. Then answer the questions. Mark the space for the answer you have chosen.

Station #39

Each year our class <u>takes</u> a field trip to visit the town's fire station. We all climb inside the fire truck and explore. Rick pretends to turn on the siren. Jesse tries on a firefighter's hat. Rosa plays with the fire station's dog, Trixie. Chris slides down the fire pole. Then, the fire chief usually tells us about fire safety. We always enjoy our visit to the fire station!

2. Who is Jesse?
   ○ the fire chief
   ○ the fire station's dog
   ○ the author
   ○ a student in the class

3. In the first sentence, the word <u>takes</u> means _____
   ○ goes on
   ○ plans
   ○ grabs
   ○ walks to

Read the selection. Then read each questions. Decide which answer is best. Mark the space for the answer you have chosen.

The New Kid

1 My family moved to a new neighborhood. I didn't know anyone there. I was the new kid on the street. Mom said, "Go outside and play. You'll meet some kids. Pretty soon you'll have some friends."

2 I said to Mom, "But I don't know how to make friends."

3 "Don't worry. It will just happen," she said.

4 I went outside and saw some children playing. I looked over at them.

5 They shouted, "Come join us!"

1. In paragraph 1, which word means a place where people live?
- ○ city
- ○ neighborhood
- ○ street
- ○ outside

2. This story is mostly about –
- ○ going outside
- ○ making new friends
- ○ children playing
- ○ a new neighbor

Name _____ Date _____

Key Words

Use with Student Edition pages 72–73.

| dinner |
| well |
| roars |
| reflection |

A. **Find the Key Word from the box that completes each sentence. Write the word.**

1. We dug a _____
to find water.

2. A dog barks, but a lion _____.

3. When you look in the mirror you see your
_____.

4. We eat _____ at six o'clock in the evening.

B. **Read each clue. Find the Key Word in the row of letters. Then circle the word.**

5. meal in the evening   t w e d i n n e r v t i o n

6. hole with water   p d f l p i t a l w e l l

7. makes a loud noise   p w d w n r o a r s o l p e

8. an image of yourself   d a r e f l e c t i o n h x

Academic Words

Use with Student Edition page 74.

A. Read each clue. Find the Academic Word in the row of letters. Then circle the word.

1. pay attention to   k f o c u s o i n t e r a c t l i t

2. tell what something is   o u i d e n t i f y i g d o m

B. Read each sentence. Write *TRUE* or *FALSE*.

3. It is easy to identify someone in the dark.

_____

4. It is good to focus in class. _____

5. My glasses help me focus better. _____

6. You can identify an animal by its paw prints.

_____

C. Answer the questions.

7. What helps you **focus** in class?

_____

8. How can you **identify** a bird? Name two ways.

_____

Home-School Connection

Write a story using the Academic Words. Share your story with a family member.

Name _____ Date _____

Phonics: Long Vowel Pairs

Use with Student Edition page 75.

> The long **o** sound can be spelled *oa* or *oe*.
> The long **u** sound can be spelled *ue* and *ui*.

A. Unscramble the letters to write a word that has a long **o** or long **u** sound. Then circle the letters that spell the long vowel sound.

1. _____ t b a o

2. _____ r i u f t

3. _____ e c u l

4. _____ o t e

B. Use one of the vowel pairs to complete each word in the chart. Look back at page 75 in your Student Edition for help.

Words with long *o*	Words with long *u*
5. s _____ _____ k	**7.** c _____ _____
6. f _____ _____	**8.** s _____ _____ t

Copyright © 2019 Pearson Education, Inc.

🏠 **Home-School Connection**   Add two words to each column in the chart. Share your words with a family member.

Comprehension: *The Rabbit and the Lion*

Use with Student Edition pages 76–79.

Answer the questions about the reading.

Recall

1. Who did Lion catch?

_____

2. What does Lion see in the well?

_____

3. What does Lion hear?

_____

Comprehend

4. Why does Lion jump into the well?

_____

_____

Analyze

5. Why does Rabbit laugh at Lion?

_____

_____

_____

Name _____ Date _____

Reader's Companion

Use with Student Edition pages 76–79.

The Rabbit and the Lion

Narrator: Rabbit is smart. But one night his foe, Lion, catches him.

Rabbit: Help!

Lion: I have you now, Rabbit! I am going to eat you for dinner!

Rabbit: I am too small. You need a big animal to eat.

Lion: Yes. But you are just the right size for a snack.

Rabbit: Who are you to go around eating rabbits?

Lion: I am king of this forest!

Rabbit: Look at the lion in the well. He says he is king!

Use What You Know

List two things you like to eat for a snack.

1. _____

2. _____

Reading Strategy

MARK THE TEXT

What does Rabbit say to try to trick Lion? Underline Rabbit's words.

Comprehension Check

Circle the two words that mean *something* to eat.

MARK THE TEXT

Use the Strategy

Lion catches Rabbit. What is the first thing Rabbit does? What is the second thing?

_____

_____

_____

Retell It!

Retell this passsage as if you were Rabbit.

_____

_____

_____

_____

Reader's Response

What would you do if Lion caught you?

_____

_____

_____

Home-School Connection   Retell the passage to a family member.

Name _____ Date _____

Learning Strategies: Events in a Plot

Use with Student Edition pages 80–81.

Read the passage. Then underline five important events.

The Lion and the Mouse

Narrator: A lion catches a mouse.

Mouse: Please let me go! Someday I will help you.

Lion: You? What could you do for me?

Narrator: The lion laughed so hard he let the mouse go.
The next day, a hunter caught the lion.
The hunter tied the lion to a tree.

Lion: ROAR!

Mouse: I will chew through the rope.

Narrator: The mouse chewed through the rope and set the
lion free.

Home-School Connection | Write a story. Tell about three events. Tell the events in order. Share your story with a family member.

Grammar: Pronouns and Possessives

Use with Student Edition pages 82–83.

A pronoun takes the place of a noun. Use possessive pronouns or possessive noun ('s) to show ownership.

Subject Pronouns		Possessive Pronouns	
I	it	mine	its
you	we	yours	ours
he/she	they	his/hers	theirs

A. Complete each sentence with the correct pronoun.

1. Does this hat belong to my sister Eva? Yes, it is _____.
_____ wears it when it is sunny.

2. Does this game belong to the students? Yes, it is _____.
_____ like to play the game together.

3. Does the piano belong to Mr. Chen? Yes, it is _____.
_____ plays the piano every night.

B. Write the correct possessive pronoun on the line.

4. That coat belongs to Miss Smith. _____ coat is red.

5. The train has loud whistles. The _____ whistles are loud.

6. The crayons belong to John. Those are _____ crayons.

Home-School Connection Write two sentences about someone in your family. Use a pronoun in one of the sentences. Read the sentences to your family.

Name _____ Date _____

Spelling: Similar Words
Use with Student Edition pages 84–85.

Use with Student Edition pages 84–85.

Read each word and its definition. Then write the word that *best* completes each sentence.

> **Spelling Tip**
> Some words are easy to mix up, such as *lion* and *line*.

of	part of something
off	away from something
than	used to compare two things
then	next

1. Hector gets _____ the bus.

2. Josie is taller _____ Eddie.

3. First, we cook and _____ we eat.

4. Lion is king _____ the forest.

 Make up a rule to help you remember how to spell two similar words. Write your rule.

_____

_____

_____

 **Home-School Connection** **Read your rule to a family member.**

Writing: Write a Plot Summary

Read the paragraph. Then read each question. Circle the letter of the correct answer.

> Bruno Silva
>
> "The Lion and the Rabbit"
> By Ed Young
> (1) One night, Lion catches Rabbit. (2) Lion wants to eat Rabbit, but Rabbit trick Lion. (3) He tells Lion to look in the well. (4) Lion sees another lion in the well. (5) He shouts, "I is the king of the forest." (6) He hears his echo: "I am the king of the forest." (7) Lion is angry. (8) He jumps into the well. (9) Now Rabbit is safe.

1. What change, if any, should be made to sentence 2?
   A Change *wants* to *want*
   B Change *eat* to *ate*
   C Change *trick* to *tricks*
   D Make no change

2. What change, if any, should be made to sentence 5?
   A Change *I* to *me*
   B Change *is* to *am*
   C Change *king* to *King*
   D Make no change

3. What change, if any, should be made to sentence 6?
   A Change *his* to *him*
   B Change *hears* to *hear*
   C Change *echo* to *ecco*
   D Make no change

Name _____ Date _____

Key Words

Use with Student Edition pages 86–87.

clouds

stronger

spiders

webs

brighter

A. Find the Key Word in the box that completes each sentence. Write the word.

1. The dark _____ moved across the sky.

2. I am _____ than my little brother.

3. Flies were caught in the spider _____.

4. All _____ have eight legs.

5. Sunlight is _____ than moonlight.

B. Unscramble the letters to form a Key Word.

6. g r e b t h i r _____

7. r i p s d e s _____

8. s l u d o c _____

9. b s e w _____

10. t r g e r s n o _____

Copyright © 2019 Pearson Education, Inc.

51

Academic Words

Use with Student Edition page 88.

A. **Read each clue. Find the Academic Word in the row of letters. Then circle the word.**

1. produce a change   k f o c u s o i n t a f f e c t

2. way of thinking   a f o u a t t i t u d e o m

B. **Read each sentence. Write _TRUE_ or _FALSE_.**

3. A positive **attitude** is important. _____

4. A teacher likes a student with a bad **attitude**. _____

5. The sun can **affect** the growth of a plant. _____

6. Studying can **affect** your grades. _____

C. **Answer the questions.**

7. What are two ways to have a good **attitude** in class?

   _____

8. How does a rainy day **affect** you?

   _____

Home-School Connection   Write two sentences with the Academic Words. Share your sentences with a family member.

Name _____ Date _____

Word Study: Prefixes and Suffixes

Use with Student Edition page 89.

> The prefix *dis* means *not*. The suffix *less* means *without*.

A. Write the word from the box that *best* completes each sentence.

careless	dishonest	dislike	fearless

1. My dad is not afraid of anything. He is _____.

2. It is _____ to tell a lie.

3. The boys are scared of spiders. They _____ them a lot!

4. You do not care about doing your homework. You are _____.

B. Match each word with its definition. Write the letter of the correct answer.

5. _____ disagree   **A** without pain

6. _____ hopeless   **B** not obey

7. _____ disobey   **C** not agree

8. _____ thoughtless   **D** without hope

9. _____ painless   **E** without thinking

Home-School Connection

Write a sentence using a word with a *dis* prefix. Write a sentence using a word with a *less* suffix. Share your sentences with a family member.

Comprehension: *The Contest*

Use with Student Edition pages 90–97.

Answer the questions about the reading.

Recall

1. Who was in the contest?

_____

2. Who won the contest?

_____

3. What does the woman do?

_____

Comprehend

4. How does the North Wind help the woman?

_____

_____

Analyze

5. What lesson does this story teach us?

_____

_____

_____

Name _____   Date _____

Reader's Companion

Use with Student Edition pages 90–97.

The Contest

The North Wind took another breath and then she blew very hard. She blew leaves from the trees. She pushed flying birds from the sky. They hid in their nests. The North Wind threw spiders to the ground. She sent their webs flying away.

In the strong wind, it was hard for the woman to stay on her feet. But she never let go of her hat. She held it on her head with both hands.

Use What You Know

List two things you know about the wind.

1. _____

2. _____

Reading Strategy

Underline a sentence that describes how the wind blows.

Comprehension Check

Circle two things the North Wind did when she blew very hard.

55

Use the Strategy

Describe how you picture the North Wind blowing very hard.

_____

_____

_____

Retell It!

Retell this passage as if you were one of the spiders.

_____

_____

_____

_____

_____

Reader's Response

What would you do in such a strong wind?

_____

_____

_____

Home-School Connection   Retell the passage to a family member.

Name _____ Date _____

Learning Strategies: Visualize

Use with Student Edition pages 98–99.

Read the passage. Then describe pictures you make in your mind.

The Race

Today there is a race in my town. All the children can enter. I want to win the race. I know I am a fast runner. I want to beat Annie. She thinks she is faster than me.

We go to the starting line. The coach says, "Ready, set, go!" I move fast. Soon I am in front of everyone. I can hear someone running close behind me. She catches up, and I see it is Annie.

Annie and I run as fast as we can. We cross the finish line. The coach says, "It is a tie." Annie and I both get medals.

"You are fast," Annie says to me.

"Yes, but you are fast, too," I tell her.

1. What picture do you have of the person telling the story?

_____

_____

2. How do you picture Annie?

_____

_____

Home-School Connection Ask a family member to tell you a story. Visualize as you listen. Draw a picture of one part of the story.

Grammar Simple Past (Regular Verbs)

Use with Student Edition pages 100–101.

Use the simple past to talk about a completed action that happened before now. Make the simple past of regular verbs by adding *-ed*.

Add *-d* to verbs ending in *-e*.	move ⟶ moved
Change the **y** to *i* and add *-ed* to verbs ending in the consonant *-y*.	cry ⟶ cried
Add *-ed* to verbs ending in a vowel and *-y*.	play ⟶ played
Double the consonant and add *-ed* for verbs with a stressed CVC ending.	stop ⟶ stopped

A. Change the verb to the past. Write your answer on the line.

1. walk   The boys _____ to school yesterday.

2. play   Maria _____ on the swings at recess.

3. cook   Dad _____ meat on the grill.

4. jump   Anna and Sarah _____ rope together.

5. shout   The children _____ in excitement.

B. Use the verb and fill in the blanks to make negative statements.

6. close   She _____ the window.

7. ask   You _____ the question last week.

8. laugh   The boys and girls _____ at the joke.

9. rain   It _____ last night.

Home-School Connection   Make a list of five verbs in the past. Read them to your family.

Name _____   Date _____

Spelling: The Long *u* Sound

Use with Student Edition pages 102–103.

Read each clue. Write the word that matches the clue. Then circle the letters that spell the long *u* sound.

blue	clue	crew	few	new

1. a group on a space shuttle _____

2. the color of the sky _____

3. the opposite of *old* _____

4. a hint _____

5. not many _____

 Write three sentences using long *u* words.

_____

_____

_____

_____

Home-School Connection Make a list of words with the long *u* sound. Share your list with a family member.

Writing: Retell a Familiar Story

Read the paragraph. Then read each question. Circle the letter of the correct answer.

> Carmen Delgado
>
> (1) Hair laughed at slow Tortoise. (2) "I can beat you in a race," he said. (3) Tortoise answer, "Let's race and see." (4) They started the race. (5) Hare hopped away. (6) He chased butterflies. (7) Then he stopped under a trees and rested. (8) Tortoise just walked and walked. (9) Later, Hare arrived at the finish line. (10) Tortoise was already there.

1. What change, if any, should be made to sentence 1?
   A Change *laughed* to *laugh*
   B Change *Hair* to *Hare*
   C Change *Tortoise* to *tortoise*
   D Make no change

2. What change, if any, should be made to sentence 3?
   A Change *answer* to *answered*
   B Change *see* to *saw*
   C Change *Let's* to *lets*
   D Make no change.

3. What change, if any, should be made to sentence 7?
   A Change *stopped* to *stops*
   B Change *under* to *in*
   C Change *trees* to *tree*
   D Make no change.

Name _____   Date _____

Key Words

Use with Student Edition page 104–105.

farm

fresh

grow

plants

garden

A. **Find the Key Word in the box that completes each sentence. Write the word on the line.**

1. The vegetables were _____ because we just picked them.

2. My neighbors planted a _____ near their house.

3. We bought seeds to _____ flowers and vegetables.

4. Our tomato _____ are higher every time we measure them.

5. A _____ is a place where people grow food, even on a building.

B. **Circle four Key Words in the Word Search.**

P	C	X	D	W	M	R	F
G	A	R	D	E	N	B	F
M	D	R	F	P	F	S	R
G	H	B	A	R	H	O	E
A	R	T	R	Z	D	N	S
R	T	T	M	I	X	R	H
D	X	P	L	A	N	T	S
E	S	H	Y	J	N	G	H

Academic Words

Use with Student Edition page 106.

A. Read each clue. Find the Academic Word in the row of letters. Then circle the word.

1. communicate   k m o p i n t e r a c t f r p l

2. result   d o u t c o m e t l d m p

B. Read each sentence. Write *TRUE* or *FALSE*.

3. When you work with others you interact. _____

4. Not studying can result in a poor grade. _____

5. Birds often interact with dogs. _____

6. Most winning teams have a poor outcome. _____

C. Answer the questions.

7. How do you **interact** with your friends?

   _____

   _____

8. What are two **outcomes** of studying hard?

   _____

   _____

Home-School Connection   Write a paragraph telling what you know about how plants grow. Share your paragraph with a family member.

Name _____ Date _____

Phonics: More Long Vowel Pairs

Use with Student Edition page 107.

The sound of long *a* can be spelled *ay* or *ai*.
The sound of long *e* can be spelled *ee* or *ea*.
The sound of long *i* can be spelled *ie*.

A. List the words by the long vowel sounds. Then circle the letters that make each vowel sound. The first one is done for you.

clean	cried	hay	pie	rain
seed	skies	stay	week	

Long *a* Pairs	Long *e* Pairs	Long *i* Pair
h(ay)	_____	_____
_____	_____	_____
_____	_____	_____

B. Use a vowel pair to make a word with the long vowel sound.

1. n _____ d

2. l _____

3. c l _____

4. _____ t

5. t r _____ n

6. n _____ t

Home-School Connection   Make a list of two words for each long vowel pair. Share your list with a family member.

Comprehension: *Fresh Food in Strange Places*

Use with Student Edition pages 108–113.

Answer the questions about the reading.

Recall

1. How is the world's population changing?

_____

2. What is an urban farm?

_____

3. What happens to the food that people grow on an urban farm?

_____

Comprehend

4. Why do people need new places to grow their fresh food?

_____

_____

_____

Analyze

5. How can growing fresh food help people get along?

_____

_____

_____

Name _____ Date _____

Reader's Companion

Use with Student Edition pages 108–113.

Fresh Food in Strange Places

As cities get bigger and bigger, there are fewer farms. It is hard for people in big cities to get fresh food. People in big cities use urban farms on buildings and city parks. It looks strange, but it's a great idea. The urban farmers sell their fresh food in their community.

Many schools around the world also have their own gardens and grow their own food. These schools use the food to feed students. Starting a farm or a garden can help the whole neighborhood.

Use What You Know

List three unexpected places to grow food.

1. _____

_____

2. _____

_____

3. _____

_____

Reading Strategy MARK THE TEXT

Circle a sentence in the second paragraph that is an opinion.

Comprehension Check

Circle two words that mean people living together. MARK THE TEXT

Use the Strategy

List two facts from the passage.

_____

_____

_____

Retell It!

Retell this passage. Pretend you are asking someone at your school to start a garden at the school. What would you tell them?

_____

_____

_____

_____

Reader's Response

Where would you grow food if your community needed more fresh food? Write the names of the places on the lines.

_____

_____

_____

Home-School Connection   Retell the passage to a family member.

Name _____ Date _____

Learning Strategies: Identify Fact and Opinion

Use with Student Edition pages 114–115.

Read the passage. Then answer the questions.

Mom and Dad had a good idea. They wanted to plant a garden for fresh food for the community. They needed help. They asked the neighbors. Everyone liked the idea of a garden. The neighbors decided to name the garden. They named it Old Orchard Garden.

Dad made a list of jobs. The neighbors signed up for the jobs. Some people dug the soil. Others pulled the weeds. And other people planted the seeds. They planted lettuce, beans, tomatoes, corn, and peas. I helped water the plants. That was the best job.

1. Find an opinion. Write it on the line.

_____

_____

2. What garden job would you like best?

_____

_____

Home-School Connection Write a sentence about how a garden can help a community. Share your sentence with a family member.

Grammar Simple Past: *Be* Verbs

Use with Student Edition pages 116–117.

The past *be verb* tells about events that started and finished in the past. *Be* verbs must agree with the subject.

Subject	Past
I	was
He/She/It	was
You/They/We	were

A. Write a *be* verb in the past tense on each line.

1. We _____ at my grandparents' farm last weekend.

2. She _____ at my house yesterday.

3. I _____ very busy last week.

4. My brothers _____ at a basketball game last night.

B. Complete the *Yes/No* questions and the answers with the simple past form of *be*.

5. _____ you home last night? No, I _____.

6. _____ she here today? Yes, she _____.

7. _____ I late this morning? No, you _____.

8. _____ we in the same game yesterday? Yes, we _____.

Home-School Connection Make a list of *be* verbs. Read them to your family.

Name _____ Date _____

Spelling: Long *a* Spelling Patterns

Use with Student Edition pages 118–119.

A. **Make a word with a long *a* spelling pattern.**

1. m _____	**4.** p _____ d
2. w _____	**5.** w _____ t
3. s _____	**6.** _____ t

> **Spelling Tip**
>
> The letters *ai* and *ay* make the long *a* sound. The letters *eigh* also can make the long *a* sound, as in **neighbor**.

eight	hay	neigh	neighborhood	trail

B. **Fill in the blanks with a word from the box. Use each word once.**

   I like go to the horse farm in my _____ .
I visit the four horses in the field. Then I go into the stable. I pet
the four horses inside. There are _____ horses
on the farm. The farmer brings _____ to feed
the horses. They _____ . Later, I get to ride a
horse on the _____ .

  Write about your neighborhood. Use words with *ai*, *ay*, and *eigh*.

_____

_____

 **Home-School Connection** Make a list of six long *a* words that rhyme. Share your list with a family member.

Writing: Write a Journal Entry about Your Day

Read the paragraph. Then read each question. Circle the letter of the correct answer.

> Wednesday, January 15th
>
> (1) I wasn't in School yesterday. (2) This morning, my techer put a math test on my desk. (3) Suddenly I was nervous. (4) I couldn't think. (5) My brain was frozen. (6) My teacher asked, "Are you OK." (7) But I couldn't move. (8) I was scared. (9) Then my teacher smiled. (10) She said, "You weren't here yesterday. (11) Don't worry. (12) I'll help you."

1. What change, if any, should be made to sentence 1?
   A Change *I* to *me*
   B Change *School* to *school*
   C Change . to *?*
   D Make no change

2. What change, if any, should be made to sentence 2?
   A Change *techer* to *teacher*
   B Change *put* to *puts*
   C Change *my* to *mine*
   D Make no change

3. What change, if any, should be made to sentence 6?
   A Change *teacher* to *Teacher*
   B Change *asked* to *asking*
   C Change . to *?*
   D Make no change

Name _____   Date _____

Review

Use with Student Edition pages 66–119.

Answer the questions after reading Unit 2. You can go back and reread to help find the answers.

1. In *The Rabbit and the Lion*, which event happens last? Circle the letter of the correct answer.
   A Lion says he is king of the forest.
   B Lion jumps into the well to fight.
   C Lion roars loudly at his reflection.
   D Rabbit tells Lion to look in the well.

2. Read these sentences from *The Rabbit and the Lion*.

   Narrator: Lion looks into the well. He sees a lion in the water.
   Rabbit: Ha! Ha! He thinks his own reflection is another lion!

   What is a *reflection*?

   _____

   _____

3. Describe how you picture the Sun in *The Contest*.

   _____

   _____

4. Read this sentence from *The Contest*.

> The birds peeked out of their nests.

What does *peeked* mean? Circle the letter of the correct answer.

A cried   **C** sang

B fell   **D** looked

5. How is the Sun in *The Contest* like Rabbit in *The Rabbit and the Lion*?

_____

_____

6. In *Fresh Food in Strange Places*, why do people need to grow food in new places?

_____

_____

7. What is true about urban farms? Circle the letter of the correct answer.

A People use parks or buildings in big cities for urban farms.

B People have large animals on urban farms.

C Urban farms need a lot of land.

D Urban farms are only in one part of the world.

Home-School Connection   Tell a family member something new you learned from this unit.

Name _____ Date _____

Writing Workshop: Write a Story

Read the passage. Then read each question. Circle the letter of the correct answer.

(1) My birthday was last weak. (2) I had a birthday surprise. (3) Some visitors came to my party. (4) They were not invited.

(5) That morning Mom baked my birthday cake. (6) She iced the yellow cake with chocolate icing. (7) I was excited. (8) The cake looked beautiful. (9) Mom said "I will put candles on the cake."

(10) Mom invited the neighbors to my party. (11) She went to the kitchen. (12) I heard Mom scream. (13) I run into the kitchen. (14) "Look!" Mom said. (15) I saw a row of ants. (16) They were marching across my cake. (17) We decided to buy a new cake at the bakery.

1. What change, if any, should be made to sentence 1?
   A Change *weak* to *week*
   B Change *birthday* to *Birthday*
   C Change *was* to *is*
   D Make no change

Circle the letter of the correct answer.

2. What would be the **best** way to combine sentences 3 and 4?

   A Some visitors came to my party since they were not invited.

   B Some visitors came to my party because they were not invited.

   C Some visitors came to my party but they were not invited.

   D Some visitors came to my party so they were not invited.

3. What change, if any, should be made to sentence 9?

   A Change *put* to *puts*

   B Change Mom said *"I will put candles on the cake."* to Mom said, *"I will put candles on the cake."*

   C Change *cake* to *cakes*

   D Make no change

4. What change, if any, should be made to sentence 13?

   A Change *run* to *ran*

   B Change *run* to *runned*

   C Change *into* to *from*

   D Make no change

5. What change, if any, should be made to sentence 14?

   A Change to: *!* to *?*

   B Change to: *Look!* to *"Look!"*

   C Change to: *Mom* to *mom*

   D Make no change

Name _____ Date _____

Fluency

Use with Student Edition page 127.

How fast do you read? Use a clock. Read *Fresh Food in Strange Places*. How long did it take you? Write your time in the chart. Read three times.

Many schools around the world also have their	8
own gardens, and grow their own food. In school	17
gardens, students learn about science while they	24
grow vegetables and fruits. They also learn how to	33
work together. The school then uses the produce	41
to feed students in the school. Many students like	50
trying the food that they grow!	56

My Times

Learning Checklist

Check off what you have learned well. Review if needed.

Word Study and Phonics

☐ Long Vowel Pairs
☐ Prefixes and Suffixes
☐ More Long Vowel Pairs

Strategies

☐ Events in a Plot
☐ Visualize
☐ Identify Fact and Opinion

Grammar

☐ Pronouns and Possessive Nouns
☐ Simple Past: Regular Verbs
☐ Simple Past: *be* Verbs

Writing

☐ Write a Plot Summary
☐ Retell a Familiar Story
☐ Write a Journal Entry about Your Day
☐ Writing Workshop: Write a Story

Listening and Speaking

☐ Perform a Skit

Name _____ Date _____

Test Preparation

Use with Student Edition pages 128–129.

Read this selection. Then answer the questions below. Mark the space for the answer you have chosen.

Prickly Pears

The desert can be a challenging place to live. But the prickly pear cactus is a tough plant! Although the desert only gets a few inches of rain each year, prickly pears can grow to be up to 10 feet tall. Prickly pears have special leaves that store water to keep them healthy in very hot and dry weather. These plants are also covered with sharp, yellow spines to protect them from predators.

1. Which part of a prickly pear cactus helps protect it from animals?

   ◯ leaves   ◯ water

   ◯ pears   ◯ spines

2. Which of the following sentences is an opinion?

   ◯ The prickly pear cactus is a tough plant!

   ◯ Prickly pears can grow to be 10 feet tall.

   ◯ Prickly pears have special leaves that store water.

   ◯ These plants are covered with sharp, yellow spines.

Read the selection. Then read each questions. Decide which answer is best. Mark the space for the answer you have chosen.

A School Garden

1 Some schools have gardens. They grow vegetables like lettuce, beans, and tomatoes. The teachers show the children what to do.

2 First, the children get the soil ready. Then they plant the seeds. They must water the garden and pull the weeds. Gardens are a lot of work.

3 Other things grow in the garden besides vegetables. The children grow too. They grow by learning to work together. They learn to get along. A garden is a great way to learn.

1. In paragraph two the word soil means –

○ gardens

○ plant

○ dirt

○ weeds

2. What do children learn by working in a garden?

○ to like vegetables and other plants

○ to work hard at school

○ to grow weeds and pull them

○ to grow plants and work together

Name _____ Date _____

Key Words

Use with Student Edition pages 136–137.

amazing

camels

caves

habit

plains

A. Choose the best Key Word from the box. Write the word on the line.

1. Flat grassy lands are called _____.

2. You can find bats in _____.

3. _____ live in the desert.

4. Some animals can do _____ tricks.

5. Exercising regularly is a good _____.

B. Write the Key Word that best matches the clue.

6. Animals with humps _____

7. Surprising _____

8. Act performed regularly; routine _____

9. Flat grasslands _____

10. Opening in the earth where bats live _____

Academic Words

Use with Student Edition page 138.

A. **Read each clue. Find the Academic Word in the row of letters. Then circle the word.**

1. like or understand the value of something

k m a p p r e c i a t e s l

2. show

d g a r d p l i l l u s t r a t e

B. **Read each sentence. Write TRUE or FALSE.**

3. Not saying thank you shows that you appreciate something. _____

4. A how-to book illustrates how something is done. _____

5. The photos illustrate how the animal looks. _____

6. If you appreciate your friends, you ignore them. _____

C. **Answer the questions.**

7. How would you **illustrate** where bats live?

_____

8. How do you show that you **appreciate** someone who did something nice for you?

_____

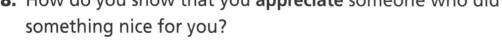

Home-School Connection Tell a family member about your favorite animals. Use the Academic Words.

Name _____ Date _____

Phonics: Consonant Clusters

Use with Student Edition page 139.

In **clusters,** the sounds of both letters blend together.

r-blends	*l*-blends	*s*-blends
br, cr, dr, fr, gr, pr, tr	bl, cl, fl, gl, pl, sl	sc, sk, sm, sn, sp, st, sw

Add an *r*-blend, *s*-blend, or an *l*-blend to make a word.

1. _____ oom

2. _____ ile

3. _____ ee

4. _____ ape

5. _____ ay

6. _____ ess

7. _____ eep

8. _____ ip

9. _____ ue

10. _____ im

Home-School Connection

Write three sentences using some of the words you made. Share your sentences with a family member.

Comprehension: *Animal Habitats, Alligators and Crocodiles*

Use with Student Edition pages 140–143.

Answer the questions about the reading.

Recall

1. What are some animals that live in the ocean?

_____

2. How are the heads of alligators and crocodiles different?

_____

3. Which animal has one tooth that sticks out, an alligator or
a crocodile?

_____

Comprehend

4. Why do animals live in different habitats?

_____

_____

Analyze

5. Why do you think so many animals live in an ocean habitat?

_____

_____

Name _____   Date _____

Reader's Companion

Use with Student Edition pages 140–143.

Animal habitats can be found all around us;
In caves and water, with flat plains and trees.
Animals live where their needs can be met.
They can roam wherever they please.

The rainforest is a hot and rainy place.
It is home to half of the world's creatures.
Sloths and snakes call this place home.
The rainforest has unusual features.

The desert is a place where it's hot and dry.
No animal, it seems, could ever survive here for long.
This habitat is full of creatures, big and small —
But snakes, camels, and foxes all seem to belong!

Use What You Know

List the animals that live in the desert.

1. _____

2. _____

3. _____

Reading
Make Inferences

Circle the sentence that tells us the rainforest is a good place to study animals.

Comprehension Check

Circle two words that are habitats to different animals.

Use the Strategy

Why can most animals not live in the desert for long?

_____

_____

_____

Retell It!

Retell the passage as if you lived in the rainforest.

_____

_____

_____

_____

_____

Reader's Response

What animal would you like to be? Write about where you would live.

_____

_____

_____

Home-School Connection Retell the passage to a family member.

Name _____ Date _____

Learning Strategies: Inferences

Use with Student Edition pages 146–147.

Read the passage. Put a check by the sentence that _best_ tells what you can figure out by reading.

Parents

Mother and father birds have a lot to do. First they have to build the nest. Then they have to sit on the eggs until they hatch. But their work is not done. Baby birds need to be fed. The parents bring the babies worms to eat. Sometimes people or animals get too close to the nest. The parent birds will squawk to keep them away.

_____ Lots of animals like to eat birds.

_____ Birds do a good job of caring for their young.

_____ Birds do not care much for their young.

_____ Birds teach their babies how to fly.

Home-School Connection With a family member, make a list of birds and other animals you have seen.

Grammar: Prepositions of Location

Use with Student Edition pages 148–149.

A **preposition** is always followed by a noun or pronoun.

Preposition of Location	Prepositional Phrases
in	**in** caves
on	**on** the floor
at	**at** school
between	**between** the table and the wall
near	**near** the fence
under	**under** the sea
above	**above** the door

A. Complete the sentence with the *best* preposition of location. Write your answer on the line.

1. The boys climbed _____ the fence.

2. Molly sat _____ the swing.

3. Dad put his coat _____ the closet.

4. The bus stop is _____ my house.

5. The clouds float _____ the Earth.

6. We had a carnival _____ school.

7. I put some jam _____ two slices of bread.

B. Underline the prepositional phrase in each sentence above.

Home-School Connection

Take a coin and a box. Put the coin *in, on, near, under, above* the box. Have your family guess the preposition.

Name _____ Date _____

Spelling: Adding -ing

Use with Student Edition pages 150–151.

Change the underlined word to the -ing form. Rewrite each sentence.

1. I am <u>make</u> a poster about animals.

_____

2. Are you <u>share</u> your toys?

_____

3. The bears are <u>live</u> in caves.

_____

4. We are <u>hike</u> in the hills.

_____

5. She is <u>write</u> a letter to her grandmother.

_____

Write two sentences about what animals do. Use words that drop the silent *e* to add *-ing*.

_____

_____

Home-School Connection Share your sentences with a family member. Explain the rule.

Writing: Write a Poem about an Animal

Read the poem. Then read each question. Circle the letter of the correct answer.

---

(1) I am a bat.

(2) I am as blak as night.

(3) I live in caves or in treetops.

(4) I eat insects or fruit.

(5) I slept upside down during the day with other bats.

(6) I can fly through the air.

(7) I see in the dark.

(8) I am a bat.

---

1. What change, if any, should be made to sentence 2?

A Change *night* to *knight*

B Change *am* to *is*

C Change *blak* to *black*

D Make no change

2. What change, if any, should be made to sentence 3?

A Change *live* to *lives*

B Change *in treetops* to *on treetops*

C Change *caves* to *cave*

D Make no change

3. What change, if any, should be made to sentence 5?

A Change *slept* to *sleep*

B Change *day* to *night*

C Change *upside* to *inside*

D Make no change

Name _____   Date _____

Key Words

Use with Student Edition pages 152–153.

insect

habitats

camouflage

prey

patterns

moth

A. Choose the Key Word from the box that *best* completes each sentence. Write the word.

1. Some butterflies have colorful

_____ on their wings.

2. Rivers and lakes are

_____ for fish.

3. A bird is a cat's _____ .

4. A _____ looks a lot like a butterfly.

5. That _____ looks like a stick!

6. Rabbits use _____ to stay safe.

B. Match each Key Word with its definition. Write the letter of the correct answer.

7. _____ habitats   **A** what animals use to hide

8. _____ moth   **B** animals' homes

9. _____ camouflage   **C** animal that other animals eat

10. _____ prey   **D** small flying insect

Academic Words

Use with Student Edition page 154.

A. Read each clue. Find the Academic Word in the row of letters. Then circle the word.

1. land, sea, air   l p e l e n v i r o n m e n t a l p r a t

2. to help someone   d g i l e n a b l e e s v o n m e n t l

B. Read each sentence. Write TRUE or FALSE.

3. People and animals live in an environment.   _____

4. The environment for fish is the land.   _____

5. Most students learn in a good school environment.   _____

6. A dictionary will enable me to use a map.   _____

C. Answer the questions.

7. What is a good **environment** for an alligator?

_____

8. What **enables** the bat to fly?

_____

Home-School Connection Explain to a family member how animals use camouflage to stay safe.

Name _____   Date _____

Word Study: Compound Nouns
Use with Student Edition page 155.

> **Compound words** are made up of two shorter words.
>
> something   classroom   birthday
> some / thing   class / room   birth / day

Read each clue. Then use the words in the box to write the compound word.

note	boat	bow	brush
bed	grass	hopper	house
board	skate	rain	set
sun	tooth	room	book

1. you use it to brush your teeth _____

2. an insect that can jump very high _____

3. it is flat and rolls on wheels _____

4. a home that is on the water _____

5. you might see this after it rains _____

6. where you might sleep _____

7. this is what you write in _____

8. this happens at the end of a day _____

Home-School Connection   Think of five compound words. Use each one in a sentence. Share your sentences with a family member.

Comprehension: *Can You See Them?*

Use with Student Edition pages 156–159.

Answer the questions about the reading.

Recall

1. What animal looks like a branch?

   _____

2. Why do animals hide?

   _____

3. What word describes how animals hide?

   _____

Comprehend

4. Without camouflage, what would happen to some animals?

   _____

   _____

   _____

Analyze

5. What happens to animals when their habitats are destroyed?

   _____

   _____

Name _____ Date _____

Reader's Companion

Use with Student Edition pages 156–159.

Can You See Them?

Arctic foxes live where the weather is very cold. They can change color. In summer, the foxes are brown. In winter, they are white.

A tawny frogmouth is a bird. It sits very still in a tree. It waits for prey to come near. Then it pounces!

Patterns help this moth stay safe. Look at the big spots on the moth's wings. They look like a large animal's eyes. Predators stay away from this insect.

A Bengal tiger is a very large cat. It's hard for a big animal to hide. But the tiger has stripes. When it rests in the forest, its stripes blend in with the plants.

Use What You Know

List two things you know about animals.

1. _____

2. _____

Reading Strategy

MARK THE TEXT

Find three causes and effects in the passage. Write *C* over the cause. Write *E* over the effect.

Comprehension Check

What is a tawny frogmouth?

_____

_____

_____

Use the Strategy

Why do you think Arctic foxes are a different color in summer than in winter?

_____

_____

_____

Retell It!

Retell one part of the passage as if you were a park ranger telling about an animal in your park.

_____

_____

_____

_____

Reader's Response

Which of the animals in this passage would you like to learn more about? Why?

_____

_____

_____

Home-School Connection   Retell the passage to a family member.

Name _____ Date _____

Learning Strategies: Cause and Effect

Use with Student Edition pages 160–161.

Read each passage. Write the cause and effect.

Jarrett Goes to School

It was a nice day. Jarrett decided to ride his bike to school. On the way to school, he rode over a nail. One of his tires went flat. Jarrett couldn't ride the bike with a flat tire. He had to walk the rest of the way to school. He got there ten minutes late.

Cause _____

Effect _____

Lucas and Shadow

Lucas has a kitten named Shadow. Shadow is very good at hiding. Lucas taught Shadow to come when he called his name. One day, Shadow was hiding. Lucas could not find him. Then he called his name. Shadow came running.

Cause _____

Effect _____

Home-School Connection Explain cause and effect to a family member. Give an example from the selection.

Grammar: Adjectives and Adverbs

Use with Student Edition pages 162–163.

Adjectives describe nouns. They tell about size, shape, color, and number.

Adverbs answer the question *how*. Many adverbs end in *-ly*.

Adjectives		Adverbs	
a **big** box	**two** months	walked **carefully**	ran **quickly**
the **red** balloon	the **square** paper	tiptoed **quietly**	moved **fast**

A. Read each sentence. Circle the adjectives.

1. The fox ran across the big field.

2. The monkey climbed the tall tree.

3. I ate three cookies.

4. The green caterpillar sat on the leaf.

5. She picked the round package.

B. Read each sentence. Underline the adverbs.

6. The clouds moved quickly across the sky.

7. Mother sang softly to the baby.

8. Tomas and Ivan talked quietly.

9. The crowd cheered loudly for the team.

Home-School Connection

Pick out your favorite toy. Think of five adjectives that describe it. Read your adjectives to your family. Have your family guess the toy.

Name _____ Date _____

Spelling: Compound Words

Use with Student Edition pages 164–165.

Spelling Tip

To spell compound words, spell each shorter word first.

**Unscramble the shorter words.
Write the compound word.**

1. n w e s   p p r a e   _____

2. s s r o c   k l w a   _____

3. m e s o   g h n i t   _____

4. c r e a s   w r o c   _____

5. r i a   n l e p a   _____

6. n s u   s e r i   _____

7. g r e n f i   l n i a   _____

8. y d a   r e m a d   _____

✎ **Write a story. Use three of the compound words.**

_____

_____

_____

_____

Home-School Connection   **Share your story with a family member. Point out the compound words.**

Writing: Write a Friendly Letter

41 Oak Road

Bigtown, MD 09050, U.S.A.

(1) Dear grandma,

   (2) I learned about a really interesting insect in school today. (3) Have you ever seen a walking stick. (4) It is an insect that looks exactly like a tree branch or twig. (5) It uses camouflage, so birds can't find it. (6) A walking stick moves very slowly. (7) Amazingly, it can walk on water! (8) It have claws and suction cups on its feet, so it can walk upside down. (9) Isn't that cool?

Love,

Ahmed

1. What change, if any, should be made to the greeting (1)?

  A Change *grandma* to *Grandma*

  B Change *Dear* to *dear*

  C Change *,* to *!*

  D Make no change

2. What change, if any, should be made to sentence 3?

  A Change *seen* to *see*

  B Change *Have you* to *You have*

  C Change *.* to *?*

  D Make no change.

3. What change, if any, should be made to sentence 8?

  A Change claws and suction cups to claw and suction cup

  B Change *have* to *has*

  C Change *its* to *it's*

  D Make no change.

Name _____   Date _____

Key Words

Use with Student Edition pages 166–167.

butterfly
leaf
hatch
caterpillar
chrysalis
tadpole

A. **Choose the Key Word from the box that** *best* **completes each sentence. Write the word.**

1. The _____ flies from flower to flower.

2. A _____ builds

   a _____ around itself.

3. When a _____ grows up, it is a frog.

4. In autumn the _____ will turn red.

5. The baby birds _____ out of their shells.

B. **Read each clue. Find the Key Word in the row of letters. Then circle the word.**

6. part of a plant   t w s d f n t e l e a f m n

7. insect with a long body
   and large wings   p e b u t t e r f l y p e

8. insect with a round body
   and many legs   c a c a t e r p i l l a r e g

9. baby frog   s e r f u t e t a d p o l e

10. come out of an egg   d h a t c h j r t i o n h x

Academic Words

Use with Student Edition page 168.

A. **Read each clue. Find the Academic Word in the row of letters. Then circle the word.**

1. completely change   l p e l e n l n m e n t r a n s f o r m

2. happens   e n o c c u r s l a p d r i c o n m e h

B. **Read each sentence. Write TRUE or FALSE.**

3. Leap year occurs every four years.   _____

4. A tadpole will transform into a butterfly.   _____

5. A full moon occurs every night.   _____

6. A rooster will transform into a hen.   _____

7. My birthday occurs every year.   _____

C. **Answer the questions.**

8. What **occurs** each year in the spring?

   _____

9. What could you do to **transform** a bedroom?

   _____

   _____

Draw the life cycle of a butterfly. Write labels and captions.
Share your picture with a family member.

Name _____   Date _____

Phonics: Digraphs *ch*, *sh*, *th*

Use with Student Edition page 169.

> The letters *ch*, *sh*, and *th* are **digraphs**.
> Each digraph stands for one sound.

A. Circle the digraph in each word.

1. chick

2. ship

3. gather

4. munch

5. thing

B. Add *ch*, *sh*, or *th* to make a word.

6. _____ _____ o e

7. a n o _____ _____ e r

8. _____ _____ a n k s

9. t o u _____ _____

10. r u _____ _____

Home-School Connection Think of two more words each with *ch*, *sh*, and *th*.
Read your words to a family member.

Comprehension: *How Do They Grow?*

Use with Student Edition pages 170–173.

Answer the questions about the reading.

Recall

1. Where is a good place for a butterfly to lay eggs?

   _____

2. Where do frogs lay eggs?

   _____

3. What two ways do frogs move?

   _____

Comprehend

4. How are caterpillars and tadpoles alike?

   _____

   _____

Analyze

5. What is the difference between the life cycles of butterflies and frogs?

   _____

   _____

   _____

Name _____   Date _____

Reader's Companion

Use with Student Edition pages 170–173.

How Do They Grow?

A butterfly must find a place to lay eggs. A leaf is a good place.

Soon an egg will hatch. A tiny caterpillar crawls out. The caterpillar starts to eat right away. It munches on plants.

Next, the caterpillar builds a chrysalis around itself. The chrysalis sticks to a tree branch. It hangs there and does not move. But changes happen inside.

Then the butterfly breaks out of the chrysalis. It spreads its wings. It is ready to fly.

Use What You Know

List two insects you see outside.

1. _____

2. _____

Reading Strategy

Find four steps in a butterfly's life. Write the numbers 1, 2, 3, and 4 next to each step.

Comprehension Check

Where does the butterfly lay eggs? Circle the answer.

Use the Strategy

What does the caterpillar do?

_____

_____

_____

Retell It!

Tell how the butterfly grows and changes. Explain the steps as if you are the teacher in a science class.

_____

_____

_____

_____

Reader's Response

Think of different butterflies that you have seen. What did they look like?

_____

_____

_____

Home-School Connection   Retell the passage to a family member.

Name _____ Date _____

Learning Strategies: Steps in a Process

Use with Student Edition pages 174–175.

Read each passage. Then number the steps in the correct order.

Life Cycle of a Robin

First, the mother robin lays eggs in a nest. Next, the eggs hatch. The babies have no feathers. They stay in the nest. The mother brings them food. Then the young robins grow feathers and learn to fly. They leave the nest and fly away.

_____ The eggs hatch.

_____ The mother robin lays eggs.

_____ The young robins grow feathers and learn to fly.

_____ The babies have no feathers. They stay in the nest.

Life Cycle of a Frog

First, a frog lays eggs in water. Soon, the eggs hatch. Tiny tadpoles come out of the eggs. These tadpoles live in water and have no legs. One day, they start growing legs. After ten weeks, the legs are big. The tadpole can go onto land. The tadpole has become a frog.

_____ Tadpoles start growing legs.

_____ A frog lays eggs in water.

_____ The tadpole has become a frog.

_____ Tadpoles come out of the eggs.

Home-School Connection Tell a family member what you did after school today. Tell the steps in order.

Grammar: Adverbs of Time

Use with Student Edition pages 176–177.

Adverbs of time tell the order in which actions happen.

Adverbs of Time		Examples
now	later	**Tomorow** I will finish my project.
early	again	I'll see you **later**.
today	before	Let's come here **again**.
tomorrow	soon	The caterpillar will **soon** become a butterfly.

A. Read each sentence. Circle the adverbs of time.

1. We woke early in the morning.

2. Mother said she would be home soon.

3. We will study for the test later.

4. Now is the time to solve the problem.

B. Unscramble each sentence. Write it in the correct order.

5. Have a math test we later will.

_____

6. Bus soon our be here will.

_____

Home-School Connection

Describe what you plan to do over the next few days. Use adverbs of time to tell about your plans. Read your description to your family.

Name _____ Date _____

Spelling: Spelling with *tch*

Use with Student Edition pages 178–179.

Add *tch* to make each word.

1. A hu_____ is a home for rabbits.

2. My dad will make a ba_____ of cookies.

3. Pi_____ the ball to the batter.

4. Can you ma_____ the words and the pictures?

5. I will look at my wa_____ to see what time it is.

6. It rained hard. The di_____ is full of water.

7. Let's wa_____ the soccer game.

8. Can you draw or ske_____ the butterfly?

 Write a story about a child who catches a big fish. Use words with *tch* in your story.

_____

_____

_____

_____

_____

Copyright © 2019 Pearson Education, Inc.

Home-School Connection Read the sentences to a family member. Talk about what each word means.

Writing: Write a Personal Narrative

Read the paragraph. Then read each question. Circle the letter of the correct answer.

Maki Umenoto

The Day I Lost My First Tooth

(1) I lose my first baby tooth last week. (2) I felt the tooth loosen. (3) I moved it with my tongue. (4) I ran but showed my mother. (5) The next day, I put my tongue where my loose tooth was. (6) I knew that it would fall out soon. (7) Later that day, I was eating a sandwich. (8) I felt for my loose tooth again, but it was gone! (9) My mother and me looked everywhere for it. (10) Finally, I found it. (11) It was in my sandwich!

---

1. What change, if any, should be made to sentence 1?
   A Change *tooth* to *teeth*
   B Change *my* to *mine*
   C Change *lose* to *lost*
   D Make no change

2. What change, if any, should be made to sentence 4?
   A Change *show* to *shows*
   B Change *but* to *and*
   C Change *ran* to *run*
   D Make no change

3. What change, if any, should be made to sentence 9?
   A Change *everywhere* to *somewhere*
   B Change *me* to *I*
   C Change *looked* to *looks*
   D Make no change

Name _____ Date _____

Review

Use with Student Edition pages 130–179.

Answer the questions after reading Unit 3. You can go back and reread to help find the answers.

1. In *Animal Habitats*, what animals live in the ocean? Circle the letter of the correct answer.
   A camels, snakes, and foxes
   B penguins and whales
   C sloths and snakes
   D fish, sharks, coral, and sea otters

2. Read this sentence from *Alligators and Crocodiles*.

   Alligators prefer **fresh water**, crocodiles swim in the sea.

   Most of the water in the world is salt water. Which animal do you think has spread to more places, alligators or crocodiles?

   _____

   _____

3. Read these sentences from *Can You See Them?* Then write the cause and the effect.

   The cottontail rabbit hides in some leaves on the ground in the forest. It must hide from predators.

   Cause _____

   Effect _____

4. What is a *habitat*? Circle the letter of the correct answer.

A an animal's home   **C** a camouflage

B an animal's habit   **D** a predator

5. In *How Do They Grow?*, what steps does a frog go through as it grows? Circle the letter of the correct answer.

A tadpole, egg, frog

B egg, caterpillar, frog

C egg, tadpole, frog

D egg, chrysalis, tadpole

6. Where does a tadpole live?

_____

_____

7. Read these sentences from the selection.

> Soon an egg will hatch. A tiny caterpillar crawls out.

What does *hatch* mean? Circle the letter of the correct answer.

A close up   **C** crawl out

B break open   **D** fly away

8. What step is the same for both frogs and butterflies?

_____

_____

Copyright © 2019 Pearson Education, Inc.

Home-School Connection Tell a family member something new you learned from this unit.

Name _____ Date _____

Writing Workshop: Write a Personal Narrative

Read the passage. Then read each question. Circle the letter of the correct answer.

Pat Waters

On Stage

(1) This summer I was in a opera. (2) It was *Hansel and Gretel*. (3) The opera was in a big theater.

(4) I tried out for the part. (5) I sang a song. (6) Then I had to dance. (7) The director liked my song and dance. (8) He said, "you can be in the opera." (9) I was very excited.

(10) The next day I got a costume. (11) The director showed me mine part. (12) I practiced over and over again.

(13) The night of the opera I was nervous. (14) The director said, "You will be fine." (15) The curtain opened. (16) I sang my song. (17) Then I dance around the stage. (18) The audience cheered. (19) I was very happy.

1. What change, if any, should be made to sentence 1?

    A Change *summer* to *Summer*

    B Change *a* to *an*

    C Change *was* to *is*

    D Make no change

2. What change, if any, should be made to sentence 8?
   A Change *said,* to *said*
   B Change *in* to *on*
   C Change *you* to *You*
   D Make no change

3. What change, if any, should be made to sentence 11?
   A Change to: *showed* to *show*
   B Change to: *mine* to *my*
   C Change to: *me* to *I*
   D Make no change

4. What is the *best* way to combine sentences 15 and 16?
   A The curtain opened because I sang my song.
   B Since the curtain opened I sang my song.
   C The curtain opened until I sang my song.
   D The curtain opened and I sang my song.

5. What change, if any, should be made to sentence 17?
   A Change *dance* to *danced*
   B Change *around* to *under*
   C Change *the* to *a*
   D Make no change

Name _____ Date _____

Fluency

Use with Student Edition page 187.

How fast do you read? Use a clock. Read the text about animals that hide. How long did it take you? Write your time in the chart. Read three times.

Many insects, birds, and other animals hide. They may	9
hide to keep safe from predators. Or, they may hide so	20
that they can catch prey. This kind of hiding is called	31
camouflage. When animals have camouflage, they are	38
hard to see in their habitats. Arctic foxes, for example,	48
live where the weather is very cold.	55
They can change color. In winter, the foxes are white.	65
In summer, they are brown. Bengal tigers are another	74
example. These big cats have stripes that help them	83
blend in with the trees and plants.	90

My Times

Learning Checklist

Check off what you have learned well. Review if needed.

Word Study and Phonics
- ☐ Consonant Clusters
- ☐ Compound Nouns
- ☐ Digraphs: *ch, sh, th*

Strategies
- ☐ Inferences
- ☐ Cause and Effect
- ☐ Recognize Sequence
- ☐ Steps in a Process

Grammar
- ☐ Prepositions of Location
- ☐ Adjectives and Adverbs
- ☐ Adverbs of Time

Writing
- ☐ Write a Poem about an Animal
- ☐ Write a Friendly Letter
- ☐ Write a Personal Narrative
- ☐ Writing Workshop: Write a Personal Narrative

Listening and Speaking
- ☐ Recite a Poem

Name _____   Date _____

Test Preparation
Use with Student Edition pages 188–189.

Read this selection. Then choose the correct words to fill in the blanks. Mark the space for the answer you have chosen.

The Traveling Tank

1 An armadillo is a small ___1___ whose back, head, legs, and tail are covered with bony plates of "armor." The name "armadillo" is a Spanish word that means "little armored one." These bands of armor give protection to the armadillo. If an armadillo feels unsafe, it will curl up into a ball until the danger is gone.

2 Armadillos have small eyes. They cannot see very well. Instead, they rely on their ___2___ sense of smell to hunt. An armadillo uses its sharp ___3___ and strong legs to dig for food. It uses its pointy snout and long, sticky tongue to find and eat all sorts of insects.

1. ○ flower
   ○ mammal
   ○ fish
   ○ tree

2. ○ weak
   ○ colorful
   ○ small
   ○ strong

3. ○ feet
   ○ face
   ○ claws
   ○ armor

Directions

Read the selection. Then read each question. Decide which answer is best. Mark the space for the answer you have chosen.

An African Adventure

1 Many people like to take pictures. It is a treat to visit Africa. There are many wild animals there. But sometimes the animals are hard to find. So visitors have to look very carefully.

2 The lions hide in the tall grasses. Their fur is yellow just like the grass. Leopards hide in the trees. Their spots are brown like tree branches. Hippos stand in lakes with just the tops of their heads and eyes showing.

3 Animals blend in with their surroundings. This is called <u>camouflage</u>. Want a picture of an animal? You will have to look carefully to find one.

1. Why do animals hide?

○ they want to find a home

○ they don't want their pictures taken

○ they want to protect themselves

○ they want to scare visitors

2. Why do some people go to Africa?

○ to hide with the animals

○ to stand in the lakes

○ to see wild animals

○ to camouflage themselves

Name _____ Date _____

Key Words

Use with Student Edition pages 196–197.

donate

volunteers

bicycles

helmets

A. Choose the Key Word from the word box that _best_ completes each sentence. Write the word.

1. The _____ made cookies to sell at the fair.

2. Many children will _____ old toys to sell.

3. Jess and Kim rode their _____ to the fair.

4. They wore _____ to be safe.

B. Unscramble the letters to form a Key Word. Then use the Key Word in a sentence.

5. n d a o e t _____

_____

6. i c l b e s c y _____

_____

7. e m s l h e t _____

_____

8. t e n o e u r l v s _____

_____

Academic Words

Use with Student Edition page 198.

A. Read each clue. Find the Academic Word in the row of letters. Then circle the word.

1. helped by   k m z b e n e f i t s g h w

2. most of the time   d b n o r m a l l y t s a f e

B. Write the Academic Word that best completes each sentence.

3. I _____ walk to school.

4. We _____ from extra practice in school.

5. She will _____ from extra study time.

6. My family _____ eats dinner at 5:00 pm.

C. Answer the questions.

7. What time do you **normally** go to bed? _____

   _____

8. What is the **benefit** of eating fresh vegetables? _____

   _____

Home-School Connection Make up your own questions using the Academic Words. Ask a family member to answer your questions.

Name _____ Date _____

Word Study: Pronunciation of Ending -ed
Use with Student Edition page 199.

Add *-ed* to a verb to show something happened in the past.

A. Write the past form of each verb.

1. load _____

2. fix _____

3. repair _____

4. hunt _____

5. learn _____

B. Read each sentence. Underline the words with *-ed* where the ending added a syllable. Circle the words with *-ed* where the ending did not add a syllable.

6. The spaceship landed on the moon.

7. I stacked the cups on the shelf.

8. Did you like how the movie ended?

9. We painted pictures in art class.

10. Jenna looked out the window.

Home-School Connection
Write five sentences using verbs ending in *-ed.*

Comprehension: *On Your Bike, Get Set, Donate!*

Use with Student Edition pages 200–205.

Answer the questions about the reading.

Recall

1. What happens to many old bikes?

_____

2. What can bicycle riders do with their old bikes?

_____

3. What happens to donated bikes?

_____

Comprehend

4. Why is it important that these groups give helmets along with the bikes?

_____

_____

Analyze

5. Why do you think people volunteer to fix bikes?

_____

_____

_____

Reader's Companion

Use with Student Edition pages 200–205.

On Your Bike, Get Set, Donate!

Young people can help, too. Joshua started fixing bikes when he was twelve years old. He gave them to children who did not have families.

Joshua got started when his own bike broke. He had an idea. He would learn how to fix it himself. Soon, neighbors were bringing old bikes to Joshua's house. He repaired them. Now other children have new bikes.

Use What You Know

List two places where you can ride bicycles.

1. _____

2. _____

Reading Strategy

MARK THE TEXT

Read the passage. In the second paragraph, circle Joshua's problem. Underline the sentence that shows how he solved the problem.

Comprehension Check

Who did Joshua give bikes to? MARK THE TEXT
Draw a box around the answer.

Use the Strategy

What problem did Joshua solve when he fixed his neighbors' old bikes?

_____

_____

_____

Retell It!

Retell the passage as if you are Joshua.

_____

_____

_____

Reader's Response

What would you like to do to help people?

_____

_____

_____

Home-School Connection Summarize the passage for a family member.

Name _____ Date _____

Learning Strategies: Problems and Solutions

Use with Student Edition pages 208–209.

Read the passage. Complete the Problem and Solution Chart.

Jamie's New Bike

Jamie's neighbor, Kara, got a bicycle. Jamie watched Kara ride it around the block.

"I wish I had a bicycle," said Jamie.

"You can have my old bike," said Jamie's big sister, Lauren. "But the front tire is flat."

Jamie had an idea. He went to Kara's house. He asked her, "Do you have a tire pump?"

"Yes," said Kara. "It is in the garage."

The two friends found the tire pump. They pumped up the front tire until it was full. Now Jamie has a new bike, too. Jamie and Kara can ride their bikes together.

Problem	Solution

 **Home-School Connection** With a family member, write about a problem you had. Tell how you solved it.

Grammar: *Need/Want + to + Verb*

Use with Student Edition pages 210–211.

Need and *want* are always followed by *to* + verb (called an *infinitive*).

Subject	Verb	Infinitive	
She	wants	**to ride**	her bike.
They	want	**to fix**	bikes.
Children	need	**to wear**	helmets.

A. Underline *need/want/like/love + to* + **verb.**

1. I need to study for the test.

2. The boys want to play football on Saturday.

3. Sofia and Lily like to visit their grandmother.

4. Elena loves to bake cookies.

5. Mom wants to fix my bike.

B. Make each sentence negative.

1. I need to practice my song today.

   _____

2. I want to hear a funny story.

   _____

Home-School Connection

Make a list of things you need to do. Then make a list of things you like to do. Read each list to your family.

Name _____   Date _____

Spelling: Adding -es to Verbs
Use with Student Edition pages 212–213.

Read each sentence. Circle the correct spelling of the verb.

1. The boy (mix / mixes) water and sand.

2. The girl (wish / wishes) she had a horse.

3. She (reach / reaches) for her hat.

4. The bee (buzz / buzzes) by the flower.

5. Sari (touch / touches) the door.

6. The woman (push / pushes) the door open.

7. The man (guess / guesses) the answer.

8. Jill (relax / relaxes) after her race.

Write three sentences using verbs with -es added.

_____

_____

_____

_____

Home-School Connection With a family member, think of one more verb for each ending, *x, s, ch, sh,* and *z.*

125

Writing: Describe a Problem and Solution

Read the paragraph. Then read each question. Circle the letter of the correct answer.

Aiza Lee

(1) Last week, I losed my red backpack. (2) I looked at home and at school. (3) I needed to find it before the weekend. (4) I had to study for too big tests. (5) My friend Aiden wanted to help me. (6) He asked me, "When did you last have it? (7) What did you do? (8) Where did you go?" (9) I thought and thought. (10) When I remembered. (11) I had it when I went to my karate class.

1. What change, if any, should be made to sentence 1?
   A Change *week* to *weak*
   B Change *losed* to *lost*
   C Change *backpack* to *back pack*
   D Make no change

2. What change, if any, should be made to sentence 4?
   A Change *I* to *me*
   B Change *had* to *has*
   C Change *too* to *two*
   D Make no change

3. What change, if any, should be made to sentence 10?
   A Change *I* to *me*
   B Change *When* to *Then*
   C Change *remembered* to *remember*
   D Make no change

Name _____ Date _____

Key Words

Use with Student Edition pages 214–215.

| instinct |
| proof |
| tool |
| scientists |
| lab |

A. Choose the Key Word from the word box that *best* completes each sentence. Write the word.

1. Some _____ study animals in their habitat.

2. A bird breaks out of its egg

   by _____ .

3. A hammer is a _____ used to build something.

4. A scientist's laboratory may be called a _____ .

5. The photograph is _____ that the dog climbed a tree.

B. Match each Key Word with its definition. Write the letter of the correct answer.

6. _____ instinct   **a.** facts that show something is true

7. _____ tool   **b.** place where experiments are done

8. _____ lab   **c.** ability you are born with

9. _____ scientists   **d.** object or machine people use to do work

10. _____ proof   **e.** people who study the natural world

Academic Words

Use with Student Edition page 216.

A. Read each clue. Find the Academic Word in the row of letters. Then circle the word.

1. unproven idea   k m z b e t h e o r y c h s a v

2. plan for doing something   d b n a p r m e t h o d s a f e

B. Write the Academic Word that best completes each sentence.

3. We used a scientific _____ for the experiment.

4. The scientist had a _____ about gravity.

5. I will experiment to prove my _____.

6. Mom has a good _____ for packing suitcases.

C. Answer the questions.

7. What **method** do you use for studying?

   _____

   _____

8. What is your **theory** on the best way to stay healthy?

   _____

   _____

Name _____ Date _____

Phonics: *R*-Controlled Vowels: *ir, er, ur*

Use with Student Edition page 217.

> The letter *r* after a vowel gives the vowel a
> new sound. The letters *ir, er,* and *ur* usually
> have the same vowel sound.

Read each clue. Write the word from the word box that matches
the clue. Then circle the letters that make the *r*-controlled vowel
sound.

burn	curved	first	girl
herd	shirt	turn	verb

1. not straight _____

2. my little sister _____

3. an action word _____

4. a piece of clothing _____

5. number one _____

6. group of deer _____

7. what fires do _____

8. go in a circle _____

Copyright © 2019 Pearson Education, Inc.

Home-School
Connection
With a family member, list two more words for each
r-controlled sound.

Comprehension: *Scientists and Crows*
Use with Student Edition pages 218–223.

Answer the questions about the reading.

Recall

1. What sound do crows make?

_____

2. Why do scientists study crows?

_____

3. What do some crows eat?

_____

Comprehend

4. What is the difference between instinct and learning?

_____

_____

_____

Analyze

5. How do we know crows are smart birds?

_____

_____

_____

Reader's Companion

Use with Student Edition pages 218–223.

Scientists and Crows

Do you ever watch crows? You may see crows fly over trees. You may see a crow sit on a power line. Maybe you hear crows call, "Caw! Caw! Caw!"

Scientists watch crows, too. They watch what crows do in their habitat. They also study crows in labs. Scientists study crows to learn more about them.

Use What You Know

List three things you know about birds.

1. _____

2. _____

3. _____

Reading Strategy

MARK THE TEXT

Read the passage. In the second paragraph, circle the main idea. Underline two details that support the main idea.

Comprehension Check

Look at the first paragraph. Draw a box around two things crows do.
MARK THE TEXT

Use the Strategy

Why do scientists study crows?

_____

_____

How do scientists study crows?

_____

_____

Retell It!

Summarize the passage as if you are a scientist.

_____

_____

_____

_____

Reader's Response

What animals do you like to watch? Why?

_____

_____

_____

Home-School Connection ⟩ Summarize the passage for a family member.

Name _____   Date _____

Learning Strategies: Main Idea and Details

Use with Student Edition pages 224–225.

Read the passage. Then fill in the Main Idea and Details Chart.

Crows Work Together

I think crows are birds that work together. I watched two crows build a nest. They each gathered sticks and grass to build it. Then the mother sat on the eggs. The father crow brought her food. Later, three baby crows hatched. When the mother went to get food, the father sat near the nest to guard the babies.

Hawks may eat baby crows. If a hawk comes near, the adult crows team up and chase him away. I think it's really neat how the crows work together.

Main Idea

Supporting Details

Home-School Connection Watch some birds with a family member. List details that you see. Write a paragraph about the birds.

Grammar: Simple Past: Irregular Verbs

Use with Student Edition pages 226–227.

A **past verb** tells what happened before now. An **irregular past verb** does not form its past by adding -*ed*. You must remember what the past form is.

Present	Past	Present	Past
come	came	drink	drank
break	broke	swim	swam
find	found	bring	brought

A. Complete the answer using the simple past.

1. Did we <u>find</u> the right room? Yes, we _____ the right room.

2. Did your brother <u>drink</u> two glasses of milk? Yes, my brother _____ two glasses of milk.

3. Did you <u>bring</u> your book to the library? Yes, I _____ the book to the library.

4. Did Charlie <u>break</u> the window? Yes, Charlie _____ the window.

B. Change each irregular verb to its past form and use it in a sentence.

1. come

_____

2. sing

_____

Home-School Connection Make a list of five irregular verbs in the past. Read them to your family.

Name _____   Date _____

Spelling: Personal Word List

Use with Student Edition pages 228–229.

Read each word. Write its definition using a dictionary.

Spelling Tip

Keep a personal word list. Write words that are hard for you to spell.

1. experiment

_____

_____

2. observe

_____

_____

3. behavior

_____

_____

 Use the words above. Write sentences about a scientist who studies an animal.

_____

_____

_____

Home-School Connection List ten words for your personal word list. They should be words you want to remember how to spell. Read the list to a family member.

Writing: Respond to Text

Read the paragraph. Then read each question. Circle the letter of the correct answer.

Christina Ramas

(1) I thought the article "Scientists and Crows" was very interested. (2) I knew that crows could brake things apart with their sharp beaks, but I didn't know they could brake apart things in different ways. (3) For example, it fly high and drop things in the street so cars will break them apart. (4) It surprised me that the crows in Japan bent the wire into hooks so they could get the food. (5) Amazing!

1. What change, if any, should be made to sentence 1?
   A Change *Crows* to *crows*
   B Change *the* to *an*
   C Change *interested* to *interesting*
   D Make no change

2. What change, if any, should be made to sentence 2?
   A Change *apart* to *a part*
   B Change *brake* to *break*
   C Change *with* to *on*
   D Make no change

3. What change, if any, should be made to sentence 3?
   A Change *it* to *they*
   B Change *so* to *when*
   C Change . to ?
   D Make no change

Name _____ Date _____

Key Words

Use with Student Edition pages 230–231.

invented

creation

solve

accident

discover

A. Choose the best Key Word from the word box. Write the word on the line.

1. Chris was surprised to _____ the new flowers in the garden.

2. We can _____ this problem if we work together.

3. A student _____ a way to make cars safer.

4. Iris worked hard to finish her _____.

5. Sometimes an _____ turns out to be a good mistake.

B. Read each sentence. Write TRUE or FALSE on the line.

1. An artist can make a creation.   _____

2. An accident is always bad.   _____

3. You can solve a friend.   _____

4. An explorer can discover new things.   _____

Academic Words

Use with Student Edition page 232.

imply	say something in an indirect way
symbol	something that stands for an idea

A. Circle the Academic Words in the word search. Each word will appear twice.

L	R	I	G	K	E	Y	S
V	S	Y	M	B	O	L	Y
D	A	D	K	P	E	N	M
E	Z	S	M	D	L	M	B
P	A	I	M	P	L	Y	O
M	C	O	S	T	U	M	L

B. Find the Academic Word that *best* matches the clue.

1. a flag _____

2. to suggest _____

C. Answer the questions.

3. What is one **symbol** you see at school?

_____

4. How could you **imply** that you want to play a certain game?

_____

Draw a picture that shows or describes each Academic Word. Ask a family member to help you label your drawings.

Name _____ Date _____

Phonics: Hard and Soft *c*

Use with Student Edition page 235.

> A **hard *c*** has a *k* sound.
>
> A **soft *c*** has an *s* sound.

because	celebrate	center	circle
come	coat	cup	spicy

A. Choose a word from the word box with a hard *c* to complete each sentence. Write the word.

1. She wore a _____ to stay warm.

2. Please _____ to the park with me.

3. I clean my room _____ I like to be neat.

4. My dad poured water in my _____ .

B. Choose a word from the word box with a soft *c* to complete each sentence. Write the word.

5. My team likes to _____ when we score
a goal.

6. Draw a _____ around the right answer.

7. My brother likes to eat _____ food.

8. There is a hole in the _____ of the web.

Home-School Connection With a family member, list three more words with a hard *c*, and three more words with a soft *c*.

139

Comprehension: *Accidental Inventions*

Use with Student Edition pages 234–237.

Answer the questions about the reading.

Recall

1. What is this story about?

_____

2. What happened when Frank Epperson left a cup of soda outside all night?

_____

3. What did Richard James invent after he saw a spring fall off a shelf?

_____

Comprehend

4. How do we know Spencer Silver and Art Fry were a good team?

_____

_____

Analyze

5. Some inventors gave their new ideas to children. Why did the inventors choose children to test their ideas?

_____

_____

Reader's Companion

Use with Student Edition pages 234–237.

Most inventions begin as an idea. Sometimes, people may want to solve one problem but discover something else. A mistake might turn into a new invention. Some accidental inventions became toys, food, and fireworks. The inventions show an accident can be a good thing.

Use What You Know

List three things that were an accidental invention.

1. _____

2. _____

3. _____

Reading Strategy: Asking Questions MARK THE TEXT

Circle the sentence that answers the question: What do the inventions show?

Comprehension Check

Underline two words that show MARK THE TEXT that someone was the first to think of an idea.

Use the Strategy

The inventions show that an accident can be a good thing. Write a question to go with that answer.

_____

Retell It!

Retell this passage as if you were an inventor.

_____

_____

_____

_____

_____

Reader's Response

What mistakes or accidents have been good in your life? Write about the good accidents.

_____

_____

_____

Home-School Connection Summarize the passage for a family member.

Name _____ Date _____

Learning Strategies: Ask Questions

Use with Student Edition pages 238–239.

Read the passage. Then answer the questions.

It was raining. My brother and I were inside. We really wanted to play hockey outside. We discovered some marbles and some pencils. I had an idea. We invented a game that used our pencils as a hockey stick to move one marble around the table.

First, we made rules. Then, we made goals. Next, we made a place to play on the table. Finally, we played our new game we called Pencil Hockey.

We liked playing the game we invented. When my friends come over, I want to play Pencil Hockey with them, too.

1. Why did the children invent a new game? Write it on the line.

_____

_____

2. What were the pencils used for?

_____

_____

Home-School Connection

Share the questions with a family member. Tell why asking these questions helps you understand the passage.

Grammar: Nouns: Common and Proper

Use with Student Edition pages 240–241.

A **proper noun** names a specific person, place, or thing. It begins with a capital letter. A **common noun** names a person, place, or thing, but it is not specific.

Proper Nouns	Common Nouns
Albert Einstein Aunt Josie	man, scientist aunt, woman
China Asia	country continent
Amazon River Golden Gate Bridge	river bridge

A. Underline each common noun. Circle each proper noun.

1. Africa

2. bird

3. month

4. Friday

5. Egypt

6. boy

7. Jules Morales

8. uncle

9. May

10. weekday

B. Write a proper noun for each common noun.

1. girl _____

2. building _____

3. city _____

4. river _____

Home-School Connection Write the names of the people in your family. Begin each name with a capital letter. Read the names to your family.

Name _____ Date _____

Spelling: The Letter *q*
Use with Student Edition pages 242–243.

Read each clue. Write the word from the word box that matches the clue.

quack	quick	quiet
square	squeak	squeeze

1. to hold something tightly _____

2. sound a duck makes _____

3. shape with four sides _____

4. not loud _____

5. very fast _____

6. sound a mouse makes _____

✏ **Write a story about a queen who makes a quilt. See how many words with *qu* you can use in the story.**

_____

_____

_____

_____

Home-School Connection With a family member, find the meanings for *squid, liquid,* and *squall.*

145

Writing: Explain a Process

Read the paragraph. Then read each question. Circle the letter of the correct answer.

Adam Jensen

(1) I'm going to make a poster for the invention fair on monday. (2) A poster can tell other people about my invention. (3) My poster will be the first thing other people see when I show my new creation. (4) Here's how I make one: (5) First, I choose a peace of heavy paper. (6) Next I make a design on the paper using markers and a ruler. (7) Finally, I put the name of my invention at the top of the paper. (8) Now I have a poster for the invention fair!

1. What change, if any, should be made to sentence 1?
   A Change *monday* to *Monday*
   B Change *poster* to *Poster*
   C Change *make* to *made*
   D Make no change

2. What change, if any, should be made to sentence 5?
   A Change *choose* to *bring*
   B Change *peace* to *piece*
   C Change *of* to *by*
   D Make no change

3. What change, if any, should be made to sentence 7?
   A Change *Finally* to *Lastly*
   B Change *at* to *in*
   C Change *name* to *named*
   D Make no change

Name _____ Date _____

Review

Use with Student Edition pages 190–243.

Answer the questions after reading Unit 4. You can go back and reread to help find the answers.

1. Name two countries in Africa that groups donate bikes to in *On Your Bike, Get Set, Donate!* Circle the letter of the correct answer.

   A Togo and Kenya
   B Ghana and Nigeria
   C Kenya and Nigeria
   D Togo and Ghana

2. People throw away their old bikes. What is a solution to this problem?

   _____

   _____

3. Why does Bicycle Exchange teach bicycle safety to children?

   _____

   _____

4. In *Scientists and Crows*, you learn that crows in Japan crack walnuts. List two ways that the crows crack the walnuts.

   _____

   _____

5. Read these sentences from *Scientists and Crows*.

Scientists know that birds do many things by instinct. For example, they learn to fly by instinct.

What does *instinct* mean? Circle the letter of the correct answer.

A something you are born knowing how to do
B something your parents teach you how to do
C something you learn by solving a problem
D something only crows know how to do

6. In *Accidental Inventions*, how did George de Mestral discover Velcro?

_____

_____

_____

7. A teacher learned Joe McVicker's wallpaper cleaner was a good *substitute* for modeling clay. What does this word mean? Circle the letter of the correct answer.

A something that is friendly
B something that takes the place of something else
C something that is a mistake
D something that is easy to find

Home-School Connection Tell a family member something new you learned in this unit.

Name _____ Date _____

Writing Workshop: Write to Compare and Contrast

Read the passage. Then read each question. Circle the letter of the correct answer.

Terry Jones

Detectives

(1) I like to read *The Hardy Boys* mysteries. (2) I like to solve mysteries, to. (3) I am brave like Frank and Joe. (4) But my father is not a famous detective. (5) He works in the grocery store.

(6) Once I had a chance to solve a mystery. (7) Just like Frank and Joe, I will look for clues. (8) I heard a noise. (9) I looked around. (10) A laughing noise was coming from the closet. (11) I thought someone was in there.

(12) Unlike Frank and Joe, I called my father. (13) He said, "I will take a look." (14) He opened the door slowly. (15) He poked around. (16) He found my Sister's toy clown. (17) Dad solved the mystery. (18) I helped too.

1. What change, if any, should be made to sentence 1?

   A Change *The* to *the*

   B Change *mysteries* to *mysterys*

   C Change . to *?*

   D Make no change

2. What change, if any, should be made to sentence 2?

   A Change *I* to *we*

   B Change *like* to *liked*

   C Change *to* to *too*

   D Make no change

3. What change, if any, should be made to sentence 7?

   A Change *will look* to *looked*

   B Change *Frank and Joe* to *frank and joe*

   C Change *like* to *when*

   D Make no change

4. What is the *best* way to combine sentences 8 and 9?

   A I heard a noise because I looked around.

   B I heard a noise but I looked around.

   C I heard a noise so I looked around.

   D I heard a noise since I looked around.

5. What change, if any, should be made to sentence 16?

   A Change *He* to *She*

   B Change *Sister's* to *sister's*

   C Change . to !

   D Make no change

Name _____   Date _____

Fluency

Use with Student Edition page 251.

How fast can you read? Use a clock. Read the text about crows. How long did it take you? Write your time in the chart. Read three times.

Can crows use tools to solve problems? Some scientists	9
in Japan wanted to find out. They studied how crows	19
eat clams. Clams are small animals that live inside a hard	30
shell. The scientists wanted to see how crows got the clams	41
out of their shells.	45
What did the crows do? First, they picked up the clams	56
with their beaks. They carried the clams high in the air,	67
and then they dropped the clams onto the ground. When	77
the shells hit the ground, they broke. The crows ate the	88
clams inside.	90

My Times

Learning Checklist

Check off what you have learned well. Review if needed.

Word Study and Phonics

- ☐ Pronunciation of Ending -*ed*
- ☐ *R*-Controlled Vowels: *ir, er, ur*
- ☐ Hard and Soft *c*

Strategies

- ☐ Identify Problems and Solutions
- ☐ Identify Main Idea and Details
- ☐ Ask Questions

Grammar

- ☐ *Need/Want* + *to* + Verb
- ☐ Simple Past: Irregular Verbs
- ☐ Nouns: Common and Proper

Writing

- ☐ Describe a Problem and Solution
- ☐ Respond to Text
- ☐ Explain a Process
- ☐ Writing Workshop: Write to Compare and Contrast

Listening and Speaking

- ☐ Give a Presentation

Name _____ Date _____

Test Preparation

Use with Student Edition pages 252–253.

Read this selection and diagram. Then answer the questions.

My Neighbor's Garden

My neighbor loves to garden. She decided to turn an empty lot into a garden. She asked the kids on the block to help her plant the garden. We planted lots of vegetables. In the summer, my neighbor asked us to help her water the garden. Soon, the garden was bursting with vegetables! My neighbor asked us to help pick the vegetables. Soon there was a block party. All the neighbors brought food they had prepared with vegetables from the garden!

Main Idea: _____		
Detail There are vegetables in the garden.	**Detail** Kids helped the lady plant the garden.	**Detail** We _____ vegetables from the garden.

1. The main idea is –

   A how kids can eat better.

   B the lady in the garden.

   C how to eat vegetables.

   D the neighborhood garden.

2. Who helped the lady?

   F her husband

   G kids from the neighborhood

   H kids from local schools

   J her sister

3. Which word belongs on the blank in the last detail?

   A eat

   B sleep

   C drive

   D hate

Read the selection. Then read each question. Decide which answer is best. Mark the space for the answer you have chosen.

The Buffalo

1 Long ago Native Americans hunted buffalo. The buffalo was very important to them. To Native Americans, the buffalo was like a "walking store." They used every part of the buffalo they killed.

2 They used the fur for clothing. They also used it for pillows. They twisted it into ropes. They made tepees, pants, shirts, and dresses from the hide. They ate the meat. They even used the bones. They used the bones for knives, arrows, and shovels.

3 Just think! When Native Americans needed to shop, they went hunting.

1. Why was the buffalo like a "walking store?"
   - ○ it was a big animal
   - ○ it had dresses and skirts
   - ○ it provided everything they needed
   - ○ there were many buffalo

2. In paragraph 2, the word <u>twisted</u> means –
   - ○ to shop at a store
   - ○ to turn or wind
   - ○ to pull
   - ○ to take off

Name _____ Date _____

Key Words

Use with Student Edition pages 260–261.

sphere
craters
billions
planets
rotates
continents

A. **Choose the Key Word from the word box that *best* completes each sentence. Write the word.**

1. Earth _____ on its axis.

2. Earth has the shape of a

_____ .

3. Earth and Mars are _____ in our solar system.

4. Africa is one of Earth's _____ .

5. There are _____ of stars in the sky.

6. There are many _____ , or large holes, on the moon.

B. **Unscramble the letters to form a Key Word. Write the word on the line.**

7. t r a s t o e   _____

8. n n n t t o c i e s   _____

9. r e h e p s   _____

10. s t e l n a p   _____

Academic Words

Use with Student Edition page 262.

A. Read each clue. Find the Academic Word in the row of letters. Then circle the word.

1. give a task   k m z b e n e f i a s s i g n w

2. made up of   d b c o n s i s t o f m a p l y r

B. Write the word that best completes each sentence.

3. My dinner will _____ meat and potatoes.

4. The teacher will _____ each student a job.

5. Each gym class will _____ exercise and a game.

6. My dad will _____ each child a room.

C. Answer the questions.

7. What jobs does your mother **assign** to you?

_____

8. What does your favorite meal **consist** of?

_____

Home-School Connection   Use each Academic Word in a sentence. Share your sentences with a family member.

Name _____ Date _____

Word Study: Synonyms and Antonyms

Use with Student Edition page 263.

> **Synonyms** are words that have the same or similar meanings.
> **Antonyms** are words that have opposite meanings.

A. Match each word with its synonym. Write the letter of the correct answer.

1. _____ begin   **A** stone

2. _____ final   **B** start

3. _____ great   **C** important

4. _____ benefit   **D** last

5. _____ rock   **E** help

B. Write the antonym for each word.

awake	fast	heavy	old	short

6. new   _____

7. tall   _____

8. slow   _____

9. asleep _____

10. light _____

Home-School Connection With a family member, think of a synonym and an antonym for *happy, little,* and *pretty.*

Comprehension: Earth and Beyond

Use with Student Edition pages 264–269.

Answer the questions about the reading.

Recall

1. What is the shape of Earth?

   _____

2. What is our nearest neighbor?

   _____

3. What does the sun give us?

   _____

Comprehend

4. Why can't we count the stars?

   _____

   _____

Analyze

5. What is the sun made of?

   _____

   _____

   _____

Name _____ Date _____

Reader's Companion

Use with Student Edition pages 264–269.

Earth and Beyond

What is the sun?

The sun is a star. Earth and the other planets orbit the sun.

Why does the sun look so big and bright?

It looks big and bright because it is closer than any other star. The sun is so bright that we can't see other stars during the day.

The sun is always glowing. So why is the sky dark at night?

Earth rotates every 24 hours. When our side of Earth faces the sun, we have day. When our side faces away from the sun, we have night.

Why is the sun so important?

The sun warms and lights Earth.

Can people visit the sun?

No! The sun is too hot.

Use What You Know

List three things that you can see in space.

1. _____

2. _____

3. _____

Reading Strategy

When is it day on Earth? When is it night? Review the text. Underline the answers.

Comprehension Check

Why can't people visit the sun? Circle the answer.

Use the Strategy

Why does the sun look so big and bright?

_____

_____

_____

Retell It!

Pretend you are a teacher on a space flight. You are teaching a science lesson from space! Summarize the passage.

_____

_____

_____

_____

_____

Reader's Response

Where would you like to go in space if you were an astronaut? Why?

_____

_____

_____

Copyright © 2019 Pearson Education, Inc.

Home-School Connection   Summarize the passage for a family member.

Name _____ Date _____

Learning Strategies: The 5W Questions

Use with Student Edition pages 270–271.

Read the passage. Then review the passage. Answer the questions.

Shining Stars

Look at the sky at night. The tiny lights are stars. Each star is many times bigger than Earth. Stars look small because they are far away.

Stars begin as clouds of gas and dust. Over time, these clouds get hotter and hotter. The gases begin to burn. As the young star heats up, it starts to shine.

1. How big are stars?

_____

2. Why do stars look so tiny?

_____

3. What are stars made of?

_____

4. When and where were you born on Earth?

_____

 **Home-School Connection** Tell a family member one more thing you learned about the sun and stars.

Grammar: Compound Sentences

Use with Student Edition pages 272–273.

To make a compound sentence, join two simple sentences that are related. Use a connecting word such as **and** or **but**. Put a comma (,) before the connecting word.

Simple Sentence	+	Simple Sentence
The sun is a star.		It is made up of hot gases.

Compound Sentence
The sun is a star, and it is made up of hot gases.

A. **Match the simple sentences that make compound sentences. Draw a line to connect them.**

1. The moon is shaped like the Earth

   A but they cannot walk on the sun.

2. Astronauts have walked on the moon

   B and people named them for things like animals.

3. Constellations of stars looked like shapes

   C and it has mountains and plains.

B. **Combine the simple sentences to make a compound sentence. Write the compound sentence.**

1. From space Earth's oceans look blue. From space Earth's continents look brown and green.

_____

_____

Copyright © 2019 Pearson Education, Inc.

Home-School Connection   Write two compound sentences. Read them to your family.

Name _____ Date _____

Spelling: Words with *ph*

Use with Student Edition pages 274–275.

Spelling Tip

In some words, the /f/ sound is spelled *ph*.

alphabet	elephant	phone
photographer	sphere	

Read each clue. Write the word that matches the clue.

1. someone who takes a picture _____

2. big animal with a trunk _____

3. equipment you use for talking _____

4. letters that make up words _____

5. round like a ball _____

Write three sentences. Use words with *ph*.

_____

_____

_____

Home-School Connection **Share your sentences with a family member.**

Writing: Write a Persuasive Paragraph

Read the paragraph. Then read each question. Circle the letter of the correct answer.

Kim Yang

(1) Learning about space is important. (2) there are many reasons why. (3) First, scientists need to know if a comet is going to hit the earth and when. (4) Second the number of people on the earth is growing too large. (5) We may to move to another planet some day. (6) Third, it is important too find out if life exists on other planets. (7) Space exploration is expensive, but it is a benefit to everyone.

1. What change, if any, should be made to sentence 2?
   A Change *reasons* to *reason*
   B Change *are* to *is*
   C Change *there* to *There*
   D Make no change

2. What change, if any, should be made to sentence 4?
   A Change *Second* to *Second,*
   B Change *is* to *are*
   C Change *too* to *two*
   D Make no change

3. What change, if any, should be made to sentence 6?
   A Change *Third* to *Thirdly*
   B Change *too* to *to*
   C Change *exists* to *exist*
   D Make no change

Name _____   Date _____

Key Words

Use with Student Edition pages 276–277.

bark

rainbow

canoe

handprints

A. Choose the Key Word from the word box that *best* completes each sentence. Write the word.

1. They crossed the lake in a wooden _____.

2. After the storm, we saw a beautiful _____ in the sky.

3. I used dried leaves and tree _____ to make a fire.

4. We left our _____ in the wet sand.

B. Read each clue. Circle the Key Word in the row of scrambled letters.

5. outer part of a tree trunk

c a p o e s b a r k b o w s i n t s

6. marks made by pressing your hands onto something soft

r o w e h a n d p r i n t s d s b k

7. rounded row of colors seen in the sky

p r e d r a i n b o w c o e b w s t

8. narrow wooden boat with pointed end

p o e r s t l b o e h d s c a n o e

Academic Words

Use with Student Edition page 278.

A. Read each clue. Find the Academic Word in the row of scrambled letters. Then circle the word.

1. following older ideas or methods

   k m z b t r a d i t i o n a l s t l

2. something unusual we observe

   d p h e n o m e n o n l y r m e n

B. Write the Academic Word that *best* completes each sentence.

3. We have a _____ holiday dinner.

4. A shooting star is a _____ .

5. An eclipse is a _____ .

6. The Native Americans performed a _____ dance.

C. Answer the questions.

7. What traditional foods do you eat during a holiday?

   _____

8. Have you ever seen a phenomenon?

   _____

 With a family member, write a story using the Academic Words.

Name _____ Date _____

Word Study: Multiple-Meaning Words

Use with Student Edition page 279.

Multiple-meaning words have more than one meaning.

Read each sentence. Look at the word in bold type. Then circle the *best* meaning for the word.

1. I hurt my **calf** when I ran the race.

> young cow
> soft back part of a leg

2. My **palm** hurt after I caught the ball.

> tree with large, pointed leaves
> inside surface of the hand

3. The **sound** was loud and scary.

> something you hear
> healthy and strong

4. I ate an **ear** of corn at dinner.

> part of the body that you hear with
> part of some plants where the grains grow

Home-School Connection

With a family member, write your own sentences with each of the multiple-meaning words.

Comprehension: *One Moon, Many Myths*

Use with Student Edition pages 280–283.

Answer the questions about the reading.

Recall

1. Where did Hina live long ago?

_____

2. Who is Baloo?

_____

3. Where did Earth Mother send her children?

_____

Comprehend

4. What heavenly body do all these myths tell about?

_____

Analyze

5. Why did people long ago make up myths?

_____

_____

_____

Name _____   Date _____

Reader's Companion

Use with Student Edition pages 280–283.

One Moon, Many Myths

A myth from India tells about the sun and the moon.

Earth Mother had two children. She loved them very much. She wanted them to live forever. So she sent her children into the sky. Her son became the sun. Her daughter became the moon.

The daughter rose into the sky. Earth Mother wanted to hug her one last time. But it was too late. She could only touch her daughter's cheek. Earth Mother left her handprints on the moon.

Use What You Know

Name one thing you see on the moon.

_____

_____

Reading Strategy   MARK THE TEXT

Compare the son and the daughter. Underline one way they are different.

Genre   MARK THE TEXT

What part of nature does this myth explain? Circle the answer.

Use the Strategy

Contrast the son and the daughter. Tell one way they are alike.

_____

_____

Retell It!

Retell the passage as if you were the son or daughter.

_____

_____

_____

_____

Reader's Response

What thing in nature do you wonder about? Tell what you would make up a myth about.

_____

_____

_____

Home-School Connection Retell the passage to a family member.

Name _____ Date _____

Learning Strategies: Compare and Contrast

Use with Student Edition pages 284–285.

Read the passage. Answer the questions.

Venus and Mars

Venus is about the same size as Earth. It is the second planet from the sun. Venus has thick clouds all around it. This planet is very hot, and it does not have water. Venus has mountains, volcanoes, and craters.

Mars is smaller than Earth. It is the fourth planet from the sun. Mars is usually cold. This planet has ice. Mars has mountains, volcanoes, and craters.

1. Compare Venus and Mars. List two ways they are similar.

_____

_____

2. Contrast Venus and Mars. List two ways they are different.

_____

_____

Home-School Connection Summarize the passage for a family member.

Grammar: Future: *be going to*

Use with Student Edition pages 286–287.

Future verbs tell what will happen in the future. There are two ways to make the future form:

> *will + base verb* = future
> I *will get* into the canoe.

> **Present form of *be* + *going to* + base verb* = future**
> She *is going to climb* the ladder.

A. Complete each sentence with the correct form of the *be* verb.

1. I _____ going to visit Grandmother.

2. Joey _____ going to play baseball Saturday.

3. Sally and Sonia _____ going to skate in the park.

4. Mom and Dad _____ going to have a party.

B. Change the verb in each sentence to show the future. Write the sentences.

1. She climbed to the top of the tree.

   _____

2. We studied the moon and the planets.

   _____

Home-School Connection   Write two sentences. Tell two things you want to do in the future. Read them to your family.

Copyright © 2019 Pearson Education, Inc.

Name _____ Date _____

Spelling: *Two*, *Too*, and *To*
Use with Student Edition pages 288–289.

Write *two*, *too*, or *to* to complete each sentence.

Spelling Tip

Two means the number 2. *Too* means "also."

Use to before an infinitive verb, a noun, or a pronoun (*to see, to the beach, to her*).

1. I will bring my games

_____ your house.

2. You need more than _____ players!

3. _____ of my friends are coming.

4. I'll teach them, _____ .

5. Can I play, _____ ?

 **Write a story using *two*, *too*, and *to*.**

_____

_____

_____

Home-School Connection Explain the meanings of *two*, *too*, and *to* to a family member.

Writing: Write a Prediction

Read the paragraph. Then read each question. Circle the letter of the correct answer.

Kaisha Okar

(1) I predict that the United states will explore the Moon next. (2) There are several things that make the Moon important for scientists. (3) Scientists learned recently that there is water on the Moon. (4) There could be enough water to fill a reservoir in Europe. (5) Also, scientists can use the Moon as a station on the way to other planets.

1. What change, if any, should be made to sentence 1?
   A Change *states* to *States*
   B Change *predict* to *predicts*
   C Change *explore* to *explores*
   D Make no change

2. What change, if any, should be made to sentence 3?
   A Change *learned* to *learn*
   B Change *recently* to *recent*
   C Change *is* to *are*
   D Make no change

3. What change, if any, should be made to sentence 5?
   A Change *Also,* to *Also*
   B Change *use* to *used*
   C Change *scientist* to *scientists*
   D Make no change

Name _____ Date _____

Key Words

Use with Student Edition pages 290–291.

space shuttle
flight
satellite
observe
spacewalks

A. Choose the Key Word from the word box that *best* completes each sentence. Write the word.

1. Astronauts wear spacesuits when they take

   _____ .

2. A space shuttle blasts off to begin its

   _____ .

3. A robot helps scientists _____ the surface of Mars.

4. Astronauts ride the _____ to get to the space station.

5. A _____ helps televisions work.

B. Match each Key Word with its definition. Write the letter of the correct answer.

6. _____ space shuttle   **A** to look closely at

7. _____ flight   **B** a trip in a space vehicle

8. _____ satellite   **C** human-made object that orbits Earth

9. _____ spacewalks   **D** spacecraft that can travel into space and back to Earth

10. _____ observe   **E** trips made by an astronaut outside a spacecraft

Academic Words

Use with Student Edition page 278.

> **emigrate**   to leave one's country to settle in another
> **significant**   important

A. Choose the Academic Word from the box that best completes each sentence. Write the word.

1. We had a _____ snowfall.

2. He will _____ to America.

3. A good report card is _____ .

4. My aunt will _____ to England.

B. Choose the Academic Word that matches the underlined word. Write the word.

5. Maria will <u>move</u> to Spain.

   _____

6. My soccer team won an <u>important</u> game.

   _____

Home-School Connection   **Write the Academic Words. Tell a family member what they mean.**

Name _____ Date _____

Phonics: *R*-Controlled Vowels: *ar, or, ore*

Use with Student Edition page 293.

> **The letter *r* changes vowel sounds.**

Read each sentence. Underline the words with the letters *ar*. Circle the words with the letters *or* or *ore*.

1. Can you throw the ball far?

2. I sat on my porch and read the story.

3. Some sports are hard to play.

4. My dog started to bark.

5. The marching band performed at the fair.

6. Eight planets orbit the sun.

7. I scored a point before you got to the game.

8. The store window was dark.

9. Every morning, I feed the horses in the barn.

10. The drivers in the cars honked their horns!

Home-School Connection Think of two words each that have the sounds *ar* and *or/ore*. Share the words with a family member.

Comprehension: *Franklin's Dream*

Use with Student Edition pages 294–299.

Answer the questions about the reading.

Recall

1. What did Franklin want to be?

_____

2. What subjects did he like in school?

_____

3. What did he become right after college?

_____

Comprehend

4. Why did Franklin need to learn English?

_____

Analyze

5. How did Franklin's education help him?

_____

_____

_____

Name _____   Date _____

Reader's Companion

Use with Student Edition pages 294–299.

Franklin's Dream

In 1980, Franklin was chosen to become an astronaut. He started to train in classrooms and in labs. After six years of training, he was ready. It was 1986, the year of *Columbia*'s flight.

Franklin would go on six more space flights. As an astronaut, he did experiments. He made spacewalks and repaired things. Franklin went on more space flights than anyone had ever gone on before.

Flying in space is exciting. But for Franklin, the sight of Earth from outer space is the best part. He says that it is very beautiful. He says that we must take care of Earth.

"Earth is humanity's spaceship and the only one we have," says Franklin. "We must protect it."

Use What You Know

List two things you would like to do in the future.

1. _____

2. _____

Reading Strategy
MARK THE TEXT

Circle three important details that you would include in a summary.

Comprehension Check

What does Franklin say is the best part of being an astronaut? Underline the answer.
MARK THE TEXT

Use the Strategy

Summarize the first two paragraphs of the passage.

_____

_____

_____

Retell It!

Retell the last two paragraphs of the passage. Pretend you are Franklin Chang-Diaz talking to a group of children.

_____

_____

_____

_____

_____

Reader's Response

Why do you think the story of Franklin Chang-Diaz is important?

_____

_____

_____

Home-School Connection   Retell the passage to a family member.

Name _____ Date _____

Learning Strategies: Summarize

Use with Student Edition pages 302–303.

Read the passage. Then write a summary of the passage.

Mars

Mars is the fourth planet from our sun. Scientists sent a robot to Mars. The robot helps us learn about this planet.

There is ice on Mars. Scientists do not know if there are any living things. Some scientists think that there may be tiny living things under the planet's surface. Others think there may be some living things under the ice.

_____

_____

_____

_____

_____

_____

Home-School Connection   **Summarize an episode of a TV show for a family member.**

Grammar: Complex Sentences: *because* and *so*

Use with Student Edition pages 304–305.

A **clause** is a group of words with a subject and a verb. You can use *because* and *so* to connect clauses. Clauses connected by *because* and *so* are called complex sentences.

> Use *because* to give a reason:
> We missed the bus *because* we were late.

> Use *so* to give a result:
> I worked hard *so* I made the team.

A. Complete each sentence using *because* or *so*.

1. I took my umbrella _____ it was raining.

2. Maria fell _____ it was slippery.

3. Joe took the key _____ he wouldn't be locked out.

4. Mom fed the baby _____ he was hungry.

B. Circle the correct word in parentheses.

1. Mrs. Smith rakes leaves (because / so) her lawn would be neat.

2. Dad put my lunch in my lunchbox (because / so) I always forget it.

3. I wanted to go to the game (because / so) I could see my favorite team play.

Home-School Connection Write a sentence with *because*. Write a sentence with *so*. Read them to your family.

Name _____ Date _____

Spelling: Long *i* Spelled *igh*

Use with Student Edition pages 306–307.

Spelling Tip

The /i/ sound can be spelled with the letters *igh*.

bright	lightning	night
right	sight	

Read each clue. Write the word that matches the clue.

1. one of the five senses _____

2. happens during a storm _____

3. shining strongly _____

4. opposite of day _____

5. correct _____

 Write a story using three words with *igh*.

_____

_____

_____

_____

Home-School Connection With a family member, write a poem using words that rhyme with *night*.

Writing: Write a Persuasive Letter

Read the letter. Then read each question. Circle the letter of the correct answer.

NASA Headquarters
Washington DC, USA

To whom it may concern:
(1) "Please consider me as a candidate for Space Camp. (2) First of all, I'm in very good physical condition. (3) I can swim very well. I am comfortable where there is no gravity. (4) Second I could build a space ship because I have experience building models. (5) Finally, I'm very good at math and science. (6) They are my favorite subject.

1. What change, if any, should be made to sentence 4?
   A Change *build* to *builds*
   B Change *a* to *an*
   C Change *Second* to *Second,*
   D Make no change

2. What change, if any, should be made to sentence 6?
   A Change *subject* to *subjects*
   B Change *They* to *it*
   C Change *are* to *is*
   D Make no change

Name _____ Date _____

Review

Use with Student Edition pages 260–307.

Answer the questions after reading Unit 5. You can go back and reread to help find the answers.

1. Review *Earth and Beyond*. What is on the surface of the moon? Circle the letter of the correct answer.

   A dust, gas, plants, animals

   B dust, mountains, craters

   C gas, asteroids, mountains

   D craters, meteors, animals

2. Review the passage about the stars. Then write what you learned about constellations.

   _____

   _____

3. Read these sentences.

   Earth is a sphere. It is a large, round ball in space.

   What does *sphere* mean? Circle the letter of the correct answer.

   A something large

   B something in space

   C something round

   D a kind of game

4. In *One Moon, Many Myths,* how did Hina get to the moon? Circle the letter of the correct answer.

    A She took a canoe.

    B She climbed a rainbow.

    C She rose into the sky.

    D Her son became the sun.

5. Compare what you learned about the moon in the myth *Baloo the Moon* and the selection *Earth and Beyond.*

_____

_____

_____

6. Review *Franklin's Dream.* Write a summary about what he did as a child. Include three important details.

_____

_____

_____

7. Why do you think Franklin was able to make spacewalks to repair things on the space shuttle?

_____

_____

_____

Home-School Connection Tell a family member something new you learned from this unit.

Name _____ Date _____

Writing Workshop: Write a Book or Movie Review

Read the passage. Then read each question. Circle the letter of the correct answer.

Sam Menendez

(1) *molly's Pilgrim* is a wonderful book by Barbara Cohen. (3) The author really describes how Molly looks and how she feels. (4) I feel like Molly is a real person and I know her.

(6) In the story the teacher asks the student's to make pilgrims. (7) Molly doesn't know what a pilgrim is. (8) Her mother make a pilgrim doll for her to take to school. (9) All the children laugh because the doll looks like a Russian girl. (10) I like the way the characters change at the end of the story. (11) Barbara Cohen really tells a good story. (12) I think you will like this story, too.

1. What change, if any, should be made to sentence 1?

   A Change *molly's* to *Molly's*
   B Change *Pilgrim* to *pilgrim*
   C Change *molly's* to *mollys*
   D Make no change

2. What change, if any, should be made to sentence 6?

   A Change *asks* to *ask*

   B Change *student's* to *students*

   C Change *Pilgrim* to *pilgrim*

   D Make no change

3. What change, if any, should be made to sentence 8?

   A Change *make* to *makes*

   B Change *her* to *she*

   C Change *take* to *took*

   D Make no change

4. What is the BEST way to combine sentences 11 and 12?

   A Barbara Cohen really tells a good story, but I think you will like this story, too.

   B Since Barbara Cohen really tells a good story, I think you will like this story, too.

   C Barbara Cohen really tells a good story, and I think you will like this story, too.

   D Barbara Cohen really tells a good story because I think you will like this story, too.

5. What change, if any, should be made to sentence 12?

   A Change *think* to *thought*

   B Change *to* to *too*

   C Change *like* to *liked*

   D Make no change

Name _____ Date _____

Fluency

Use with Student Edition page 315.

How fast can you read? Use a clock. Read the text about our solar system. How long did it take you? Write your time in the chart. Read three times.

From our home on Earth, we see the moon,	9
stars, sun, and planets. The moon is our nearest	18
neighbor. Its dusty surface changes from very hot to	27
very cold. No animals, plants, or people live there,	36
but twelve astronauts have visited it.	42
At night, we can see stars. They look like tiny	52
lights from far away, but they are giant balls	61
of hot gas. There are billions of stars, but	70
no one has visited a star. Our sun is	79
the nearest star. It is very hot, and warms	88
and lights our planet. Earth and seven other planets	97
orbit the sun.	100

My Times

☐ ☐ ☐

Learning Checklist

Check off what you have learned well. Review if needed.

Word Study and Phonics

☐ Synonyms and Antonyms
☐ Multiple-Meaning Words
☐ *R*-Controlled Vowels: *ar, or, ore*

Strategies

☐ Use Prior Knowledge
☐ The 5W Questions
☐ Compare and Contrast
☐ Summarize

Grammar

☐ Compound Sentences
☐ Future: *be going to*
☐ Complex Sentences: *because* and *so*

Writing

☐ Write a Persuasive Paragraph
☐ Write a Prediction
☐ Write a Persuasive Letter
☐ Writing Workshop: Write a Book or Movie Review

Listening and Speaking

☐ Present a TV Newscast

Name _____ Date _____

Test Preparation

Use with Student Edition pages 316–317.

Read this selection. Then answer the questions that follow it. Mark the space for the answer you have chosen.

July 20, 1969 was the first day a man walked on the moon! The mission was called *Apollo 11*. Three astronauts traveled in a spaceship for four days to reach the moon. Their names were Neil Armstrong, Michael Collins, and Edwin "Buzz" Aldrin. The main spaceship was called *Columbia*. It had a smaller ship inside. The smaller ship was called *Eagle*. The *Eagle* landed on the moon. Neil and Buzz walked on the moon. At the same time, Michael orbited the moon in the *Columbia*. When they all came back to earth, they got a hero's welcome.

1. What was the name of the mission?
- ○ *Apollo 11*
- ○ *Eagle*
- ○ *Columbia*
- ○ *Apollo 13*

2. How many astronauts walked on the moon?
- ○ one
- ○ three
- ○ two
- ○ four

3. Which is the best summary of this paragraph?
- ○ The life of Neil Armstrong
- ○ The day man first landed on the moon
- ○ The making of Apollo 11
- ○ Returning home to a hero's welcome

Read the selection. Then read each questions. Decide which answer is best. Mark the space for the answer you have chosen.

The First Astronauts

1 Two of the first <u>astronauts</u> were named Able and Baker. They were both quite tiny. They had to be. Their space ship was not very big. They rode in the nose cone of the rocket. Their flight was 16 minutes long.

2 Able and Baker were not people. They were monkeys. Monkeys went into space before people.

3 Able and Baker were not the only animal astronauts. Other animals have traveled into space. Dogs, frogs, and mice have gone, too. Animal astronauts were important for the space program. They proved that people could travel safely into space.

1. In paragraph 1, the word <u>astronaut</u> means –
- ○ monkeys
- ○ space ship
- ○ Able and Baker
- ○ space traveler

2. Why do you think people chose monkeys as astronauts?
- ○ they liked monkeys
- ○ Able and Baker were cute
- ○ monkeys are like people
- ○ they didn't bite

Name _____ Date _____

Key Words

Use with Student Edition pages 324–325.

festival

annual

advertise

schedule

supplies

A. Choose the Key Word from the box that *best* completes each sentence. Write the word.

1. Was there music and dancing

at the _____?

2. We need to buy pencils and other _____ for school.

3. We made a poster to _____ our play.

4. The spring party is an _____ event. It takes place on May 1 each year.

5. The _____ tells us what time the movie begins.

B. Read each clue. Write the Key Word that matches the clue.

6. list of events and times _____

7. happening once a year _____

8. big event _____

9. announce an event _____

10. things you need for school _____

193

Academic Words

Use with Student Edition page 326.

A. Read each clue. Find the Academic Word in the row of letters. Then circle the word.

1. happening every year   k a n n u a l c a l i t n w

2. be involved in   d b c o n p a r t i c i p a t e

B. Write the Academic Word that best completes each sentence.

3. I will _____ in the relay race.

4. The teacher wants us to _____ in class.

5. I look forward to the _____ school play each year.

C. Answer the questions.

6. What **annual** events would you like to see at your school?

    _____

    _____

7. In which school activities do you **participate**?

    _____

    _____

Home-School Connection   Use each Academic Word in a sentence. Share your sentences with a family member.

Name _____ Date _____

Phonics: Diphthongs *ou, ow*

Use with Student Edition page 327.

> **The diphthongs *ou* and *ow* have the sound you hear in *house*.**

Read each sentence. Underline the words with the diphthongs *ou* and *ow*.

1. The apple fell down onto the ground.

2. Cows and owls are animals.

3. Dad shouted "Wow!" when he saw a mouse.

4. Every scout wore a brown cap.

5. Why is the clown frowning?

6. I followed the crowd outside.

7. All of the clouds were round and puffy.

8. Kara found our book under the couch.

9. We heard a loud sound!

10. We drove south to get to town.

Home-School Connection | Make a list of the *ou* words. Make a list of the *ow* words. Read the words on your lists to a family member.

Comprehension: *Arts Festival*

Use with Student Edition pages 328–331.

Answer the questions about the reading.

Recall

1. What town holds the festival?

_____

2. Who is the art teacher?

_____

3. What does Ms. Tan want people to donate?

_____

Comprehend

4. Why does Ms. Tan ask for donations?

_____

_____

Analyze

5. Why does the art festival have many kinds of art activities?

_____

_____

_____

Name _____ Date _____

Reader's Companion

Use with Student Edition pages 328–331.

Arts Festival!

The town of Red Tree has an arts festival each year. It is called the Summer Arts Festival. All the people in the town come.

Children and adults can take art classes. They can go to a demonstration to learn how to make pottery or a collage.

Use What You Know

List two kinds of art you like to make.

1. _____

2. _____

Reading Strategy   MARK THE TEXT

What does the author tell about? Circle the answer.

Comprehension Check

Underline two things people can do at the Summer Arts Festival.   MARK THE TEXT

Use the Strategy
What is the author's purpose in writing the passage?

_____

_____

_____

Retell It!
Retell the passage. Pretend you are trying to get people to come to the Summer Arts Festival.

_____

_____

_____

_____

Reader's Response
What would you like to do at the arts festival? Why?

_____

_____

_____

Home-School Connection Summarize the passage for a family member.

Name _____ Date _____

Learning Strategies: Author's Purpose

Use with Student Edition pages 332–333.

Read the passage. Then answer the questions.

The Art Show

Dear Grandmother,

   Please come to the Woodland Art Show. It will be at Woodland Elementary School on Saturday.

   My artwork will be in the show. I have a painting of your cat, Tiger. I have a photograph of a tree, too.

   Please come see my painting and photograph.

Love,

Julio

1. What is the author's purpose?

_____

_____

2. Give two details that explain the author's purpose.

_____

_____

Copyright © 2019 Pearson Education, Inc.

Home-School Connection

Retell the passage to a family member. Explain what the author's purpose is.

Grammar: Commas

Use with Student Edition pages 334–335.

Commas are used to separate words or phrases. Commas can make writing easier to read and understand.

Dates	
• Between the day of the week and the date	Sunday, June 2
• Between the date and the year	May 14, 2019
Locations	
• Between the city and the state or province or country in an address	Buenos Aires, Argentina
• Between the city and the state or province or country in sentences	I live in La Paz, Bolivia.
Letters	
• After the greeting	Dear Aunt Fran,
• After the closing	Sincerely,
	Ellen
Series (a series consists of *three or more* items)	
• Between all items	We grew peas, corn, and wheat.

Put commas in the correct place.

1. Dear Aunt Jane

2. Sunday February 7

3. Your friend
John Malloy

4. St. Louis MO 63117

5. Mom bought bananas grapes mangoes and oranges.

6. We saw lions monkeys bears and giraffes at the zoo.

Home-School Connection Write a sentence. Tell about three things you like. Be sure to put commas in your list. Share your sentence with a family member.

Name _____ Date _____

Spelling: Words with *sch*

Use with Student Edition pages 336–337.

| schedule | scheme | scholar |
| school | schooner | |

Read each clue. Write the word that matches the clue.

1. place where children learn _____

2. type of boat _____

3. secret plan _____

4. list of when events take place _____

5. someone who knows about a subject _____

 Fill in the chart to show your schedule in school.

Time	Activity

Home-School Connection

Write a sentence using each word from the box at the top of the page. Read your sentences to a family member.

Writing: Plan a Research Report

Fill in the charts with information to prepare for your own research report.

Choose a topic. Write questions and answers about the topic.

Broad Topic	
Question:	
Answer:	
Question:	
Answer:	

Write more questions to narrow down the topic. Which one do you want as your research question?

1. _____

2. _____

3. _____

Make a research plan.

What do I want to know?	Where can I find it?

Name _____ Date _____

Key Words

Use with Student Edition pages 338–339.

puppets	
scissors	
stapler	
yarn	
buttons	

A. Choose the Key Word from the box that *best* completes each sentence. Write the word.

1. Do not run when you are

   carrying _____ .

2. I need a _____ to put
   these sheets of paper together.

3. I help my brother with the _____
   on his coat.

4. My mom helped me knit with _____ .

5. In art class, we made _____ that fit on
   our fingers.

B. Read each clue. Find the Key Word in the row of letters.
Then circle the word.

6. toys that fit over your hand
   and can be moved

   t d a p u p p e t s o b

7. used to make sweaters

   y e p p s i c a y a r n

8. used to cut paper

   p s c i s s o r s l r n

9. used to keep pieces of
   paper together

   d e r a s t a p l e r t

10. used to close shirts and coats

    b u t t o n s e d p s

Academic Words

Use with Student Edition page 340.

A. **Read each clue. Find the Academic Word in the row of letters. Then circle the word.**

1. necessary   k p r e q u i r e d e t t i n g

2. backward   d b c o n p a r r e v e r s e t

B. **Write the Academic Word that best completes each sentence.**

3. Dad put the car in _____.

4. The teacher _____ us to do homework.

5. We will _____ our direction.

6. The school _____ us to get flu shots.

C. **Answer the questions.**

7. What are you **required** to do in a school?

_____

8. Name two things that go in **reverse**.

_____

Use the Academic Words to write about an art project you would like to do. Share your writing with a family member.

Name _____ Date _____

Phonics: The Letter Y
Use with Student Edition page 341.

> At the end of a word, the **letter y** may have a long *e* sound.
> At the beginning of a word, the letter *y* acts as a consonant.

A. Fill in the blank to complete each word. Then say the word.

1. p a r t _____

2. c i t _____

3. c o m m u n i t _____

4. s i l l _____

5. h a p p _____

B. Fill in the blank to complete each word. Then say the word.

6. _____ o u

7. _____ e t

8. _____ a r d

9. _____ e l l

10. _____ o - _____ o

Home-School Connection Look up the word *community* in a dictionary. Write a sentence using the meaning of the word. Share your sentence with a family member.

Comprehension: *How to Make Puppets*

Use with Student Edition pages 342–345.

Answer the questions about the reading.

Recall

1. How long have people made puppets?

_____

2. What is the first step to make a puppet?

_____

3. What can you do with a puppet?

_____

Comprehend

4. Why must you follow directions carefully?

_____

_____

Analyze

5. Why is making a puppet a creative thing to do?

_____

_____

_____

Name _____ Date _____

Reader's Companion

Use with Student Edition pages 342–345.

How to Make Puppets

What You Will Need

white paper plates

scissors

stapler

glue

yarn

buttons

colored paper

crayons, markers, or paint

Use What You Know

List two things you could use to make eyes on a puppet.

1. _____

2. _____

Reading Strategy [MARK THE TEXT]

What can you do with the things in this list?

_____

_____

_____

Comprehension Check

Underline two things you could use [MARK THE TEXT] to make hair for the puppet.

Use the Strategy

What is your purpose for reading the passage?

_____

_____

_____

Retell It!

Retell the passage as if you were showing a friend how to make a puppet.

_____

_____

_____

_____

Reader's Response

What would you have a puppet say and do?

_____

_____

_____

Summarize the passage for a family member.

Name _____ Date _____

Learning Strategies: Reread for Details

Use with Student Edition pages 348–349.

Put a check by your purpose for reading.

1. Why would you read a cake recipe?

_____ to enjoy

_____ to learn new facts or ideas

_____ to learn how to do something

2. Why would you read an article about animals in South America?

_____ to enjoy

_____ to learn new facts or ideas

_____ to learn how to do something

3. Why would you read a mystery story?

_____ to enjoy

_____ to learn new facts or ideas

_____ to learn how to do something

4. Why would you read a billboard about a new movie?

_____ to enjoy

_____ to learn new facts or ideas

_____ to learn how to do something

Home-School Connection

With a family member, read the weather report in the newspaper. Tell what the purpose for reading it is.

Grammar: The Imperative

Use with Student Edition pages 350–351.

The **imperative sentence** gives a command or an instruction.
It usually begins with a verb.

> **Imperative Sentences:**
> Come here. Write the answer.

A. Underline each imperative sentence.

1. Drink your orange juice.

2. Sonia put on her jacket.

3. Look at your book.

4. Mom and Dad bought food at the store.

5. Help your grandmother.

6. Don't touch the artwork.

B. Read each sentence. Change it to an imperative sentence.

7. I would like you to clear the table and wash the dishes.

_____

8. I do not want you to eat cookies before dinner.

_____

Copyright © 2019 Pearson Education, Inc.

Home-School Connection
Give directions to a family member for performing a household task.
Use imperative sentences in your directions.

Name _____   Date _____

Spelling: The *j* Sound

Use with Student Edition pages 352–353.

Read each sentence. Unscramble the underlined letters to complete the missing word.

Spelling Tip

The letter *g* has the *j* sound, /dʒ/, when it is followed by an *e*, an *i*, or a *y*.

1. Diamonds, rubies, and emeralds are <u>mse</u>.

g _____ _____ _____

2. Do you get nervous when you perform on <u>etsa</u>?

_____ _____ _____ g _____

3. A <u>frafei</u> has a long neck.

g _____ _____ _____ _____ _____

4. Be <u>telne</u> with the little kitten.

g _____ _____ _____

5. The healthy lunch gave me the <u>nyeer</u> I needed.

_____ _____ _____ _____ g _____

   Write a story. Use four of the words with *g*.

_____

_____

_____

Home-School Connection   With a family member, list four more words that have the /j/ sound spelled with a *g*.

211

Writing: How to Write a Paraphrase

Fill in the charts with information to prepare for your own research report.

Choose two paragraphs from one or more of your sources. Express the ideas in your own words. Then list the source for the paraphrase.

Text from Source	Paraphrase	Source

Text from Source	Paraphrase	Source

Name _____ Date _____

Key Words

Use with Student Edition pages 354–355.

create

public

statement

cause

symbols

A. Choose the *best* Key Word from the box. Write the word on the line.

1. The children all wore green as a

_____ about

the environment.

2. The musicians performed to raise money for the

_____.

3. We put _____ on the sign to show where

the beach was.

4. Kim wants to _____ a new entrance to

her school.

5. Our class visited the _____ library.

B. Write the Key Word that *best* matches the clue.

6. an idea that people support _____

7. open to all people _____

8. to make or design something _____

9. a way to express your ideas _____

10. shapes that stand for an idea _____

Academic Words

Use with Student Edition page 356.

A. Read each clue. Find the Academic Word in the row of letters. Then circle the word.

1. a choice   a l t e r n a t i v e c a l i t n w

2. something to achieve   d b c o n g o a l r e a n a t e

B. Write the Academic Word that best completes each sentence.

3. My _____ is to read 100 books.

4. Our class _____ is to sell the most tickets.

5. Since the road is blocked we will take an _____ road.

6. You have the _____ to bring your lunch or buy it.

C. Answer the questions.

7. What is your **goal** in school this year?

_____

8. What is your **alternative** if it rains before the game?

_____

Copyright © 2019 Pearson Education, Inc.

Home-School Connection   Write a riddle for each of the Academic Words. For example, "You walk on me, but I'm not the ground. What am I?" Your soles!

Name _____ Date _____

Word Study: Multi-Syllable Words

Use with Student Edition page 357.

In a multi-syllable word, each syllable
has one vowel sound.

Read each word. Count the syllables and write the word in the correct column.

community	statement	awareness	public	popular
illustration	graffiti	traditional	symbol	

Two Syllables	_____ _____ _____
Three Syllables	_____ _____ _____
Four Syllables	_____ _____ _____

Home-School Connection Read the words in each column to a family member.

Comprehension: *Painting for the Public*

Use with Student Edition pages 358–363.

Answer the questions about the reading.

Recall

1. When did graffiti become popular in cities?

   _____

2. What plants are in Mona Caron's paintings?

   _____

3. What colors are Alex Senna's paintings?

   _____

Comprehend

4. Why would an artist choose to make public art when they want to make a statement?

   _____

   _____

Analyze

5. Why is public art usually found in big cities?

   _____

   _____

   _____

Name _____   Date _____

Reader's Companion

Use with Student Edition pages 358–363.

Artists have been creating public art for a long time. Ancient drawings on cave walls may be the first pieces of public art. In the 1960s, graffiti on buildings or on train cars became popular. Graffiti developed into public art. Some artists paint murals on the sides of buildings. Other artists take everyday objects on the streets and turn them into art.

Public artists create art for a reason. Some want to make a statement about an important cause. When artists create art in a wide-open public place, their message reaches many people. Other artists create public art to celebrate a community or culture. Still other artists want to make a rundown, empty space more lively and beautiful.

Use What You Know

List three places to find public art.

1. _____

2. _____

3. _____

Reading Strategy: Asking Questions

Circle the sentence that supports the idea that artists use public art to allow many people to see their message.

Comprehension Check

Underline the words that tell where public art first appeared.

Use the Strategy

How do you know that you can find public art you like?

_____

Retell It!

Retell the passage as if you were a public artist.

_____

_____

_____

_____

Reader's Response

What type of public art would you like to see? Write about the art you like.

_____

_____

_____

Home-School Connection Summarize the passage for a family member.

Name _____ Date _____

Learning Strategies: Draw a Conclusion
Use with Student Edition pages 364–365.

Read the passage. Then answer the questions.

I went with my dad to the city to find public art. I was excited to go. We love finding public art. Some artists create sculptures in public places. They make colorful sculptures, sculptures made all of metal, and sculptures that move. We especially like sculptures that move.

My dad's favorite sculpture is in Melbourne, Australia. The sculpture is made of musical instruments that play short songs. Anyone can make a song for the bells to play. I do not have a favorite. I like all the sculptures that I have seen. I get excited when I find a sculpture that I can interact with.

I want to make public art someday. Then I will create a moving sculpture in a city. My dad will come and see the art. My sculpture will be his favorite.

1. Why does the writer think she will see a moving sculpture on her trip?

_____

_____

2. Why will the writer probably learn to make public art, like sculptures?

_____

_____

Copyright © 2019 Pearson Education, Inc.

Home-School Connection Retell the passage to a family member.

Grammar: Quotations

Use with Student Edition pages 366–367.

A **direct quotation** shows a speaker's exact words.

Statement telling what An said:

> An said she will create the artwork.

Direct Quotation showing what An said:

> "I like to visit public parks," she said.

Use quotation marks around the words the speaker says.
The first word in a quote is capitalized.
Use a comma to separate the speaker from the quotation.

> "I like to visit public parks," he said.

A. Add quotation marks to each sentence.

1. Mom said, We must go to bed.

2. Sonia asked Dad, Will you help me?

3. I read that book, Mike said.

4. Kim said, That is my bag.

B. Change each statement into a direct quotation.

5. Jason said math was his favorite subject.

   _____

6. Sharon said she ate three cupcakes.

   _____

Home-School Connection

Ask a member of your family a question. Write their answer using quotation marks. Read the sentence to your family member.

220

Name _____   Date _____

Spelling: Spell Check

Use with Student Edition pages 368–369.

Read the sentences. Correctly spell the underlined words.

Spelling Tip

You can type your article on a computer. Use the spell check to check your spelling. But be careful. The spell check does not find everything.

1. Can you hand me the <u>sciscors</u>, please?

_____

2. The painting made a big <u>steatmint</u>.

_____

3. These flowers are <u>beautyfull</u>. _____

4. Iris likes to <u>creayte</u> stories. _____

5. Our class worked hard for the <u>caws</u>. _____

✎ **List five words you have trouble spelling. Make sure you spell each word correctly.**

_____

_____

_____

_____

_____

Home-School Connection

Ask a family member to say these words out loud: *culture, painting, attention, symbol.* Try to spell the words.

Writing: How to Use Quotations

Fill in the charts with information to prepare for your own research report.

Choose two quotations you would like to use in your report. Fill in the charts. List the source for the quotations.

Information Search	Direct Quote	Source

Information Search	Direct Quote	Source

Name _____ Date _____

Review

Use with Student Edition pages 318–369.

Answer the questions after reading Unit 6. You can go back and reread to help find the answers.

1. In *Arts Festival!*, what is the contest at the Summer Arts Festival in Red Tree? Circle the letter of the correct answer.
   A Poster-Making Contest
   B Letter-Writing Contest
   C Pottery-Making Contest
   D Puppet-Making Contest

2. Look at the poster on page 329. What is the author's purpose in making this poster? Circle the letter of the correct answer.
   A to entertain
   B to give directions
   C to persuade
   D to provide directions

3. Read these sentences from the selection.

   The town of Red Tree has an arts festival each year. This annual event is called the Summer Arts Festival.

   What does *annual* mean?

   _____

   _____

4. What is the purpose of "Painting for the Public"?

   A to provide a funny story about public art

   B to give information about art that can be found in different places

   C to persuade people to create art

   D to provide directions on how to create public art

5. Look at the sock puppet on page 346 in the Student Edition. What could you add to this puppet?

   _____

   _____

   _____

6. What types of art can you see in public places?

   _____

   _____

   _____

7. What type of public art would you like to look at? Why do you think it is so popular?

   _____

   _____

   _____

Home-School Connection Tell a family member something new you learned in this unit.

Name _____ Date _____

Writing Workshop: Write a Research Report

Read the passage. Then read each question. Circle the letter of the correct answer.

Georgia O'Keefe American Artist

(1) Georgia O'Keefe was one of the United States' best artists. (2) She painted beautiful landscapes of new mexico. (3) But her beautiful pictures of flowers are the most famous.

(4) Georgia was born on a farm in Wisconsin in 1887. (5) She took art lessons as a child. (6) Her teacher knew she had talent. (7) After high school she studied art. (8) The teacher wanted to change her style of painting. (9) For awhile she stopped painting. (10) She taught school in Amarillo Texas. (11) Then she took a summer class for art teachers. (12) The teacher did not try to change the way she painted. (13) She began to draw and paint again.

(14) Georgia's friend showed her painting to Alfred Stieglitz. (15) He was a famus photographer. (16) He really liked Georgia's drawings. (17) He asked her to come to New York City and paint. (18) She went to New York. (19) She and Alfred got married in 1924. (20) She became a successful artist.

(21) After Alfred died, she went back to New Mexico to paint. (22) She created many beautiful works of art. (23) She dies at age 98 in 1986.

1. What change, if any, should be made to sentence 2?

   A Change *she* to *her*
   B Change *landscapes* to *landscape*
   C Change *new mexico* to *New Mexico*
   D Make no change

2. What change, if any, should be made to sentence 10?

   A Change *taught* to *teached*
   B Change *Amarillo Texas* to *Amarillo, Texas*
   C Change *school* to *School*
   D Make no change

3. What change, if any, should be made to sentence 15?

   A Change *famus* to *famous*
   B Change *.* to *?*
   C Change *photographer* to *photograph*
   D Make no change

4. What is the BEST way to combine sentences 5 and 6?

   A She took art lessons as a child, while her teacher knew she had talent.
   B She took art lessons as a child and her teacher knew she had talent.
   C She took art lessons as a child, but her teacher knew she had talent.
   D She took art lessons as a child, which her teacher knew she had talent.

5. What change, if any, should be made to sentence 23?

   A Change *in* to *on*
   B Change *at* to *of*
   C Change *dies* to *died*
   D Make no change

Name _____   Date _____

Fluency

Use with Student Edition page 379.

How fast do you read? Use a clock. Read the text about making puppets. How long did it take you? Write your time in the chart. Read three times.

Follow these steps to make a great puppet.	8
1. Put two paper plates together. The top of the plates	18
should face inside. Staple the plates together around the	27
edges. Do not staple all the way around. Leave a space	38
at the bottom open.	42
2. With scissors, cut off the bottom part of the top paper	53
plate. This will make a place for you to put your hand.	65
3. Use buttons and colored paper. Use crayons, paint, or	74
markers.	75
Make eyes, a nose, and a mouth for your puppet.	85
4. Use yarn or paper to make hair or a hat. Have fun	97
with your puppet!	100

My Times

Learning Checklist

Check off what you have learned well. Review if needed.

Word Study and Phonics

☐ Diphthongs: *ou, ow*
☐ The Letter *Y*
☐ Multi-Syllable Words

Strategies

☐ Author's Purpose
☐ Identify Steps in a Process
☐ Reread for Details
☐ Draw a Conclusion

Grammar

☐ Commas
☐ The Imperative
☐ Quotations

Writing

☐ Plan a Research Report
☐ How to Write a Paraphrase
☐ How to Use Quotations
☐ Writing Workshop: Write a Research Report

Listening and Speaking

☐ Give a How-to Presentation

Name _____   Date _____

Test Preparation

Use with Student Edition pages 380–381.

Read this selection. Then choose the correct words to fill in the blanks. Mark the space for the answer you have chosen.

Banana Pops

- 1 cup yogurt
- ½ cup orange juice
- 1 medium ripe banana, cut into pieces
- 6 small paper cups
- blender

Have an adult help you measure the yogurt and juice. Have the adult cut the banana. Then put all the __1__ into a blender. Mix until smooth. Next, pour the mixture into the paper cups. Put the cups in the freezer for about 5 hours. For more variety, try using other kinds of __2__ instead of bananas.

Makes 6 servings.

It is fun to make your own after-school __3__. These banana pops are easy to make and healthy for you, too! Make sure an adult helps you!

1. ○ chocolate
   ○ dishes
   ○ ingredients
   ○ bananas

2. ○ fruit
   ○ potatoes
   ○ bananas
   ○ pasta

3. ○ homework
   ○ snacks
   ○ movies
   ○ juice

Read the selection. Then read each questions. Decide which answer is best. Mark the space for the answer you have chosen.

Neighborhood Art Festival

1 Have you ever dreamed about being a famous artist? You don't have to wait. Why not have your own public art show?

2 Ask your neighborhood friends to help. First, pick a day for your art show. Then decide where to have your show. Show paintings, photographs, and sculptures.

3 Invite your families and neighbors to the show. You may even want to sell your artwork. You can use the money to help others.

4 You might not be famous all over the world. But you will be famous in your neighborhood.

1. In paragraph 1, the word <u>public</u> means –

○ secret.

○ expensive.

○ open to everyone.

○ indoor.

2. Why is it good to ask your friends to help?

○ because a public art show is a big project

○ so your friends can have fun

○ so you can help your friends

○ because your neighborhood can become famous